CARRY IT ON!

A History
in Song
and Picture
of the
Working Men
and Women
of America

Pete Seeger and Bob Reiser

BLANDFORD PRESS
Poole · Dorset

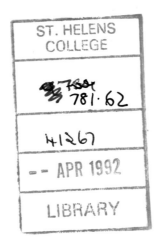
First published in the UK 1986 by Blandford Press
Link House, West Street, Poole, Dorset BH15 1LL

First published in the United States 1985 by Simon
and Schuster, a division of Simon and Schuster, Inc.,
New York.

Copyright © 1985 Pete Seeger and Bob Reiser

Distributed in Australia by
Capricorn Link (Australia) Pty Ltd
PO Box 665, Lane Cove, NSW 2066

ISBN 0 7137 1848 X (Hardback)
      0 7137 1854 4 (Paperback)

Designed by Jennie Nichols/Levavi & Levavi.
Typeset in the United States of America.

Printed in Great Britain by
Bath Press Ltd., Bath, Avon.

CONTENTS

ACKNOWLEDGMENTS

This book could never have been written without the basic research of people like American folklorists John and Alan Lomax, who found many of these songs and saved them from being lost forever; Joe Glazer, who has collected and sung labor songs for more than forty years; and Saul Schneiderman, whose magazine *Talkin' Union* is keeping union lore and history alive. We also depended on the work done by labor historians like Phil Foner, Joyce Kornbluth, Herbert Gutman, Sidney Lens, and the late William Cahn. Many of these photographs could not have been found without the valued assistance of Earl Dotter, Naomi and Walter Rosenblum, the staff of the New York University Tamiment collection, Thomas Featherstone of the Walter Reuther Library, Victoria Williams of the Amalgamated Clothing Workers, Robert Lazar of the International Ladies' Garment Workers' Union, Joe Gilmore of the United Electrical, Radio and Machine Workers of America, Joanne Delaphane of the United Mine Workers of America, and photo researcher Diane Hamilton.

We also deeply thank John Uehlein, who managed to transcribe and edit all eighty-four songs while finishing his thesis at Columbia University.

And extra thanks go to Bobbi Wayne and Claudia Carlson, who helped with some of the early designs for the book; Joy Graeme and Jay Marks, who dug through reams of paper to help us trace the copyrights on these songs; Judy Bell of TRO Music; and Harold Leventhal, who gave us office space, Xeroxing, moral support, and a dozen other kinds of help.

We have tried to track down the authors of all the songs; but authorship is often difficult to pin down. If there is anyone reading this who knows the address of someone who has not been credited, please get in touch with us.

Pete Seeger and Bob Reiser are members of the National Writers Union.

The author is grateful for permission to reprint material from the following sources:

From ''On a Note of Triumph'' by Norman Corwin, copyright 1945 Norman Corwin; copyright renewed. All rights reserved. Reprinted by permission.

From ''Chicago'' in *Chicago Poems* by Carl Sandburg, copyright 1916 by Holt, Rinehart & Winston, Inc.; renewed 1944 by Carl Sandburg. Reprinted by permission of Harcourt Brace Jovanovich, Inc.

FOREWORD

Beware! This is a book of history. With songs and pictures, we try to tell how the working people of this country—women and men; old and young; people of various skin shades, various religions, languages, and national backgrounds—have tried to better their own lives and work toward a world of peace, freedom, jobs, and justice for all.

Most of the story takes place during the last one hundred years, because of some events that came to pass in Haymarket Square, Chicago, in the early part of May 1886.

There was a nationwide strike—or as the newspapers of the day called it, a "Workmen's Holiday"—to campaign for an eight-hour workday. The factory owners, the men in power, fought with everything they could. In Chicago there was bloodshed.

However, instead of killing the labor movement, they gave it a new birthday.

The story, of course, starts earlier. When Peter Stuyvesant was governor of New Amsterdam (today's New York City) whose population was then about 3,000, the people who made a living hauling goods from the docks and delivering them to stores, warehouses, and dwellings, got their heads together one day and refused to haul more till they were paid higher wages. Stuyvesant, a tough military man, defeated them quickly, probably calling their action a conspiracy.

The haulers were probably all male and probably spoke Dutch—though not necessarily, because nineteen languages were spoken in Manhattan even then. They may have been light-skinned—though not necessarily, because "free people of color" also lived in the city.

Before that time we don't have much written history to go on. Most of the people who had been on this continent since the last Ice Age lived in small tribal villages—no rich and no poor. Maybe at times there was the equivalent of Women Strike for Peace. Maybe the wielders of stone picks and shovels among the Mound Builders laid down their tools and stood up for their rights. We'll never know.

We do know what happened in 1886. We do know it was a long time coming. Since the end of the Civil War, the Industrial Revolution had been charging ahead full speed. Some people made millions and lived in vast estates like royalty. But most people were working twelve, fourteen, and sixteen hours a day.

That is why the newly formed American Federation of Labor sent out a call for an eight-hour workday.

Across the U.S.A. more than half a million workers paraded in the streets. They had songs—hundreds of songs.

Since then people have gone on marching in the streets, talking out, striking, singing and working together for a better life.

Sometimes it seems that we have to keep fighting the same battles over and over. But every now and then the mist does rise and we can see how far we have come since the days of Governor Stuyvesant.

Each step forward came as the result of enormous work and courage, some bloodshed, and music like this which kept people's spirits alive.

As the late Lee Hays said:

"Good singing won't do;
Good praying won't do;
Good preaching won't do;
But if you get them all together
With a little organizing behind it,
You get a way of life
And a way to do it."

Keep singing.
Keep making things better.
—PETE SEEGER AND BOB REISER

CHAPTER 1

OH, FREEDOM!
1770–1865

"He'd not take his hat off to any man. Not the best of manners perhaps, but molded by the fashion of the day. You might call it Tea Party etiquette. . . . The likes of him, made the Revolution, and in making it he was changed."

—Boston journalist's description of Robert Hughes, shoemaker and participant in the Boston Tea Party

From our earliest immigrants, the Indians, to the European and African and Oriental people who transformed woods and swamp into city and field, this land has been the sum of its hardworking people.

Farmers and housewives turned the soil and built homes; boatsmen navigated treacherous waterways. Craftsmen, mill workers, plainsmen, and slaves—they built America with their hands and brains and courage.

When they joined together in the mid 1700s to help win America's independence, a new tradition was born: working together. It was one of the strengths that made this nation possible.

"[Americans] look out for mutual assistance, and, as soon as they have found one another out, they combine. From that moment, they are no longer isolated men, but a power seen from afar."

—Alexis de Tocqueville, *Democracy in America,* 1835

Again and again people have united, in guilds, in workingmen's parties, in unions, to work for a decent life.

• THE BENNINGTON RIFLEMEN •

Arranged and adapted by John Allison

Why come ye hith-er, red-coats? Your minds what mad-ness fills? In our for-ests there is dan-ger, and there's dan-ger in our hills. Hear ye not the sing-ing of the bu-gle loud and free? Full soon you'll hear the ring-ing of the ri-fle from the tree. For the ri-fle, * for the ri-fle * In our hands shall be no tri-fle. For the ri-fle, * For the ri-fle * In our hands shall be no tri-fle!

* The guitarist should knock on wood with knuckles here.
  A drummer would use "rim shots." I usually get a crowd
  of kids to clap their hands in the staccato
  —P.S.

2. Had ye no graves at home,
   far across the briny water,
   That hither ye must come
   Like bullocks to the slaughter?
      When ye meet our mountain boys
      And their leader Johnny Stark,
      Lads who make but little noise
      But who always hit the mark,
         CHORUS

3. Ye may ride a goodly steed,
   Ye may know another master,
   Ye forward come with speed,
   But ye'll learn to back much faster.
      If we the work must do,
      Then the sooner 'tis begun,
      If flint and trigger do but hold,
      The battle will be won,
         CHORUS

13

The Indians

In the woods and plains beyond the farms and the towns lived a million other people—America's first settlers: the Indians. Though few could join guilds or even get jobs, they did not escape this new industrial age. A growing America needed land. The Indians had it.

"How can you buy or sell the sky, the warmth of the land? The idea is strange to us.

"If we do not own the freshness of the air and the sparkle of the water, how can you buy them?

"Every part of this earth is sacred to my people. Every shining pine needle, every sandy shore, every mist in the dark woods, every clearing and humming insect is holy. . . .

"We are part of this earth and it is part of us. The perfumed flowers are our sisters; the deer, the horse, the great eagle, those are our brothers. The rocky crests, the juices in the meadows, the body heat of the pony, and man all belong to the same family. . . .

"The white man does not understand our ways. One portion of the land is the same to him as the next, for he is a stranger who comes in the night and takes from the land whatever he needs. The earth is not his brother, but his enemy, and when he has conquered it, he moves on. His appetite will devour the earth and leave behind only a desert. . . .

"All things are connected. Whatever befalls the earth befalls the sons of earth. If men spit upon the ground, they spit upon themselves. Contaminate your bed and one night you will suffocate in your own waste. Even the white man can not be exempt from the common destiny. We may be brothers after all. We shall see."

—Chief Seattle, 1850s

• SENECA CANOE SONG •

The song was taught to Ray Fadden by Jesse Cornplanter, a Seneca. It's important not to change it; keep that unusual extra beat (yo-ho) in the middle of the first line. Sing it high, with a good lungful of air to push it out.
—P.S.

Traditional

Ka - yo-wa - ji - neh, yo ho___ hey___ yo

ho_____ Ka - yo-wa - ji - neh, _____

Ka - yo-wa - ji - neh - eh   Ka - yo - wa - ji -

neh _____ yo ho_____ hey_____

Ka - yo-wa - ji - neh_____ Ka-yo-wa - ji - neh - eh.

The Women

"Sweep the house, dress up the dishboard and set all things in good order. Milk the kine, suckle the calves, strain the milk, take up and dress the children, provide breakfast, dinner and supper. . . . Send corn and malt to the mill for baking and brewing . . . make butter and cheese . . . feed the swine morning and evening and the poultry in the morning. Look after the hen and goose eggs. Take care of the chickens.

"Get the garden in order, keep it weeded. Sew flax and hemp for sheets, board cloths, towels, shirts, smocks, other necessities . . . Other duties are winnowing corn, washing, haymaking, harvesting, spreading manure, plow driving, loading hay or corn, going to market to sell produce and to buy all household requisites. . . ."
> —A woman's journal, late 1700s

"By her nature, her sex—a woman, like the Negro, is and always will be to the end of time, inferior . . . and therefore doomed to subjection."
> —Newspaper editorial, circa 1800

• LIFE IS A TOIL •

Anonymous, 19th century

One day I was walk-ing; I heard a com-plain-ing and saw an old wom-an, the pic-ture of gloom. She gazed on the mud on her door-step ('Twas rain-ing), and this was her song as she wield-ed her broom: "Oh, life is a toil__ and love is a trou-ble.__ Beau-ty will

fade___ and rich-es will flee. Plea-sures they

dwin-dle and pric-es they dou-ble, and noth-ing is

as I would wish it to be!"

2. "There's too much of worriment goes in a
   bonnet.
   There's too much of ironing goes into a shirt.
   There's nothing that's worth all the time you
   waste on it.
   There's nothing that lasts us but trouble and
   dirt.

   CHORUS

3. "In March it is mud; it is slush in December;
   The midsummer breezes are loaded with
   dust;
   In fall the leaves litter; in muddy September
   The wallpaper rots and the candlesticks rust.

   CHORUS

4. "With grease and with grime, from corner to
   center,
   Forever at war and forever alert,

No rest for a day lest the enemy enter,
I spend my whole life in a struggle with dirt.

CHORUS

5. "Last night in my dreams I was stationed
   forever
   On a far little rock in the midst of the sea,
   My one chance for life was a ceaseless
   endeavor
   To sweep off the waves as they swept over
   me.

   CHORUS

6. "Alas, 'twas no dream—ahead I behold it;
   I see I am helpless my fate to avert."
   She laid down her broom, and her apron she
   folded.
   She lay down and died and was buried in
   dirt.

   CHORUS

17

The Farmers

"I well remember the cold Summer [1816] when we rose on the eighth of June to find the earth covered with a good inch of newly fallen snow, when there was frost every month and corn did not fill till October. Plants grew very slowly that season while burrowing insects fed and fattened on them. My task was to precede my father as he hoed his corn, and kill the wire worms and grubs that were anticipating our harvest.

"To ride horse to plough soon became my usual vocation; the horse preceding and guiding the oxen. . . . Occasionally, the plough would strike a fast stone, and bring me and the team all standing, pitching me over the horse's head and landing me three or five feet in front. . . . Picking stones is a never ending labor. Pick as closely as you may, the next ploughing turns up a fresh eruption of boulders and pebbles from the size of hickory nuts to that of a tea kettle."
—Horace Greeley

18

"In God We Trusted. In Kansas We Busted."

—Sign on back of wagon, 1856

• THE FARMER IS THE ONE •

Author unknown

This nineteenth-century song was originally written and sung as "The Farmer Is the Man." In these days the song has taken on new life and verses and one important word change. The introduction and fourth verse are new.

—P.S.

INTRODUCTION

freely E   A

We worked through spring and win-ter, through sum-mer and through fall, But the

mort-gage worked the hard-est and the stead-iest of us all. It

worked through nights and Sun-days, through ev-'ry hol-i-day. It

set-tled down a-mong us, and it nev-er went a-way.

VERSE

Oh, the farm-er comes to town __ with his wag-on bro-ken

down, but the farm-er is the one that feeds 'em all.

If you'll on-ly look and see, I think you will a-

gree that the farm-er is the one that feeds 'em all.

CHORUS

The farm-er is the one,— the farm-er is the one.—

Lives on cre-dit till the fall; then they

take him by the hand and they lead him from the land, and the

mid-dle-man's the one who gets it all.——

2. Now the banker stands around while the
   butcher cuts a pound;
   They forget that it's the farmer feeds them
   all.
   And the preacher and the cook, they go
   strolling by the brook;
   They forget that it's the farmer feeds us all.
   The farmer is the one, the farmer is the one.
   Lives on credit till the fall.
   With the interest rates so high, it's a wonder
   he don't die,
   And the mortgage man's the one who gets it
   all.

3. Now, the banker says he's broke, and the
   merchant's up in smoke.
   They forget that it's the farmer feeds them
   all.

It would put them to a test if the farmer took
a rest;
They'd remember that the farmer feeds them
all.
The farmer is the one, the farmer is the one,
Lives on his credit till the fall.
His pants are wearing thin; his condition, it's
a sin.
They've forgot that he's the one who feeds
us all.

TAG
The farmer is the one, the farmer is the one.
Lives on his credit till the fall;

Then the taxes force his hand, and he's got
to sell his land—
And so we get a thousand shopping malls.

21

COD FISHERY

The Boatsmen

" 'Whoo-hoo! Wa-hee' screamed the leader, raising some old war whoop to the skies, as every oarsman in the strained boat involuntarily bounced forward with one tremendous leading stroke.

"His wild screams were answered by others quite as wild. 'Kee-hee Kee-hee!' yelled Daggoo, straining forwards and backwards on his seat like a pacing tiger in his cage.

" 'Ka-la koo-loo!' howled Queequeg, and thus with oars and yells the keels cut the sea."

—Herman Melville, *Moby Dick*

• GREENLAND FISHERIES •

Traditional
Adapted by John and Alan Lomax

'Twas in eight - een hun - dred and fif - ty -
three, of June the thir - teenth day
That our gal - lant ship her an - chor weighed
and for Green - land sailed a - way, brave boys, For
Green - land sailed a - way.

2. The lookout on the crosstrees stood,
A spyglass in his hand.
"There's a whale, there's a whale,
There's a whale-fish," he cries,
"And she blows at every span, brave boys,
And she blows at every span!"

3. We struck that whale, and the line payed out,
But she made a flunder with her tail,
And the boat capsized and four men were
drowned
And we never caught that whale, brave boys,
And we never caught that whale.

4. "To lose the whale," our captain cries,
"It grieves my heart full sore.
But to lose four of my gallant men,
It grieves me ten times more, brave boys,
It grieves me ten times more."

5. Oh, Greenland is a dreadful place.
It's a land that's never green,
Where there's ice and snow and the whale-
fishes blow
And daylight's seldom seen, brave boys.
And daylight's seldom seen.

The Craftsmen

Craftsmen—tinkers and shoemakers and tinsmiths—had been part of America since the 1600s. As our country grew, their numbers multiplied. By 1810, two hundred shoemakers had set up tiny ten-by-ten-foot shops in Essex, Massachusetts, and were making some of the world's finest shoes.

But our best artisans couldn't keep up with factories turning out shoes by the hundreds. Shoe prices dropped so low that the craftsmen couldn't even feed their families.

When the shoemakers of Philadelphia struck to regulate prices, the court found them "guilty of conspiracy to restrain trade." If they wanted to make any living at all, they would have to hire out as factory hands, often to the same mills that had put them out of business.

"A combination of workingmen to raise their wages . . . is to benefit themselves and to injure those who do not join their society. The law condemns both."

—Judge Moses Levy,
from shoemakers' strike decision

• PEG AND AWL •

Traditional

In the years___ of eight - een and

one,___ Peg and awl,___ In the years___

___ of eight - een and one,___ Peg and awl,___

In the years___ of eight - een and

one,___ Peg - ging shoes was all I

done.___ Hand me down___ my pegs,___ my pegs,___

___ my pegs,___ My awl.___

2. In the days of eighteen and two,
   Peg and awl,
   In the days of eighteen and two,
   Peg and awl,
   In the days of eighteen and two,
   Pegging shoes was all I'd do.
   Hand me down my pegs,
     my pegs, my pegs,
   My awl.

3. In the days of eighteen and three,
   Peg and awl,
   In the days of eighteen and three,
   Peg and awl,
   In the days of eighteen and three,
   Pegging shoes was all you'd see.
   Hand me down my pegs,
     my pegs, my pegs,
   My awl.

4. In the days of
     eighteen and four,
   Peg and awl,
   In the days of
     eighteen and four,
   Peg and awl,
   In the days of
     eighteen and four,
   I said I'd peg them
     shoes no more,
   Throw away my
     pegs, my pegs,
     my pegs,
   My awl.

5. They've invented a
     new machine,
   Peg and awl,
   They've invented a
     new machine,
   Peg and awl,
   They've invented a
     new machine—
   Purtiest little thing
     you ever seen.
   Throw away my
     pegs, my pegs,
     my pegs,
   My awl.

6. Makes one hundred
     pairs to my one,
   Peg and awl,
   Makes one hundred
     pairs to my one,
   Peg and awl,
   Makes one hundred
     pairs to my one,
   Pegging shoes, it
     ain't no fun.
   Throw away my
     pegs, my pegs,
     my pegs,
   My awl.

STRIVE TO EXCEL.

W. S. & C. H. THOMSON'S SKIRT MANUFACTORY.

The Mill Workers

In 1790, America's first factory, a textile mill, opened in Pawtucket, Rhode Island. It employed families—men to do the heavy work, wives to supervise, and children to work indoors. But children were not skilled enough to keep up with the complex machinery. "Rosy-cheeked maidens" from local farms were better.

In time, merchant capitalists bought the mills, bringing with them a new spirit—"Increase production!" Women who were operating one loom now took care of four. The ten-hour day became a twelve-hour day, a thirteen-hour day.

When a manager at the Holyoke mills in Massachusetts found that his hired hands were "languorous after eating breakfast," he solved his problem by "working them without breakfast." He was delighted when the women produced 3,000 more yards of cloth each week.

> "Give yourself no uneasiness about a deficit—we will take care of that!"
>
> —Kirk Boot, Lowell plant manager

A low black baggage wagon, the "Slaver," cruised the countryside looking for susceptible young maidens who would work in the factories.

"She . . . cruises Vermont and New Hampshire with a commander whose heart must be as black as his craft who is paid a dollar a head for all he brings to market. . . . [He is paid] more if he brings them from such a distance that they can not get back. This is done by hoisting false colors and representing to the girls that the work is neat and the wages such that they can dress in silk and spend half their time reading. Is this true? Let those girls who have been grossly deceived answer."

> —*Voice of Industry*,
>   Lowell, Massachusetts, 1846

> "The work must not be stopped! If you are not able to work, you better stay out all the time."
>
> —*Voice of Industry*, 1847

• PITY ME, MY DARLING •

Collected, adapted and arranged by John A. Lomax and Alan Lomax

No more shall I work in the fac - t'ry to greas - y up my clothes;____ No

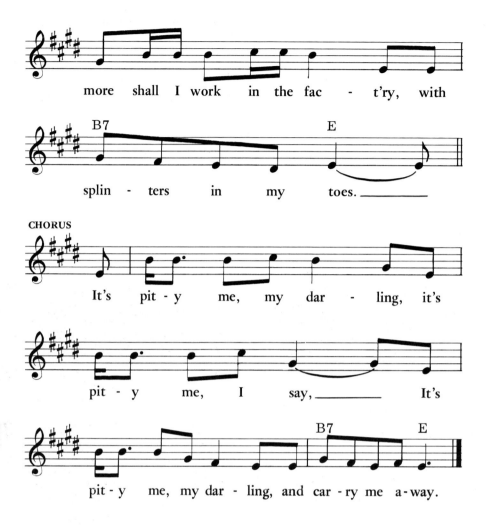

more shall I work in the fac - t'ry, with

B7   **E**

splin - ters in my toes. _____

CHORUS

It's pit - y me, my dar - ling, it's

pit - y me, I say, _____ It's

B7   **E**

pit - y me, my dar - ling, and car - ry me a - way.

2. No more shall I hear the bosses say,
   "Boys, you'd better daulf";
   No more shall I hear those bosses say,
   "Spinners, you had better clean off."
               CHORUS

3. No more shall I wear the old black dress,
   Greasy all around;
   No more shall I wear the old black bonnet,
   With holes all in the crown.
               CHORUS

4. No more shall I hear the whistle blow
   To call me up so soon;
   No more shall I hear the whistle blow

To call me from my home.
            CHORUS

5. No more shall I hear the drummer wheels
   A-rolling over my head;
   When factory girls are hard at work,
   I'll be in my bed.
               CHORUS

6. No more shall I see the super come,
   All dressed up so fine,
   For I know I'll marry a country boy
   Before the year is round.
               CHORUS

Plainsmen

Frustrated mill hands, freed slaves, even sailors like the one who changed the song

*"Oh, bury me not in the deep deep sea,
Where the dark blue waves will roll over me"*

into

*"Oh, bury me not on the lone prairee,
Where the wild coyotes will howl over me"*

went west for better opportunity—to farm or to make a fortune in gold.

But bad luck, crop failures and high debts forced many to sell their land and take back-breaking jobs as cowhands and buffalo hunters. If the hard work didn't get them there was always the food, or the trail bosses.

"It was a hell of a trip down Pease River, lasting several months. We fought sandstorms, flies, bedbugs, wolves, and Indians. At the end of the season old Crego announced he had lost money and could not pay us off. We argued the question with him. He didn't see our side of things, so we shot him and left his damned old bones to bleach where he had left so many stinking buffalo. . . ."
—Buffalo hunter, quoted by John Lomax
in *Cowboy Songs*, 1927

29

• THE BUFFALO SKINNERS •

As sung by Woody Guthrie

Am (throughout)

'Twas in the town of Jacks-bo-ro _____ in the spring of 'sev-en-ty-three, _____ A man by the name of Cre-go _____ came step-ping up to me _____ say-ing, "How do you do, young fel-low, _____ and how would you like to go _____ and spend one sum-mer pleas-ant-ly _____ on the range of the buf-fa-lo?"

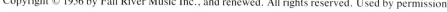

30

2. "It's me being out of employment," this to
    Crego I did say;
    "This going out on the buffalo range depends
    upon the pay.
    But if you will pay good wages and
    transportation too,
    I think, sir, I will go with you to the range of
    the buffalo."

3. "Yes, I will pay good wages, give
    transportation too,
    Provided you will go with me
    and stay the summer through;
    But if you should grow homesick,
    come back to Jacksboro,
    I won't pay transportation
    from the range of the buffalo."

4. It's now our outfit was complete—
    seven able-bodied men,
    With navy six and needle gun.
    Our troubles did begin.
    Our way it was a pleasant one,
    the route we had to go,
    Until we crossed Pease River
    on the range of the buffalo.

5. It's now we've crossed Pease River,
    our troubles have begun.
    The first damn tail I went to rip,
    Christ! how I cut my thumb!
    While skinning the damn old stinkers
    our lives they had no show,
    For the Indians watched to pick us off
    while skinning the buffalo.

6. He fed us on such sorry chuck
    I wished myself 'most dead.
    It was old jerked beef, stale coffee, and
    rotten sour bread.
    Pease River's as salty as hellfire;
    the water I could never go.
    Oh, God, I wished I had never come
    to the range of the buffalo.

7. Our hearts were cased with buffalo hocks;
    our souls were cased with steel.
    And the hardships of that summer
    would nearly make us reel.
    The fleas and graybacks worked on
    us—oh, boys, it was not slow.
    I'll tell you there's no worse hell on earth
    than the range of the buffalo.

8. The season being near over,
    old Crego he did say
    The crowd had been extravagant,
    was in debt to him that day.
    We coaxed him and we begged him,
    and still it was no go. . . .
    We left old Crego's bones to bleach
    on the range of the buffalo.

9. Oh, it's now we've crossed Pease River
    and homeward we are bound,
    No more in that hellfired country
    shall ever we be found.
    Go home to our wives and
    sweethearts, tell others not to go,
    For God's forsaken the buffalo range
    and the damned old buffalo.

The Railway Builders

"With the regularity of machinery, the workmen dropped each rail in place, spiked it down, and seized another. Behind them, the locomotive; before, the tie-layers: beyond those the graders; and still further, in the mountain recesses, the engineers. It was Civilization pressing west—the conquest of nature moving toward the Pacific."
— Newspaper account, 1868

John Henry was a real person—a black man employed digging a tunnel in West Virginia. In the Western states Chinese were the main railroad builders.

• JOHN HENRY •

Traditional

This is a version of John Henry I put together after forty years of singing it. I've used verses I got from the painter Tom Benton and others; the last verse, one of the best in the song, was discovered by Alan Lomax.

—P.S.

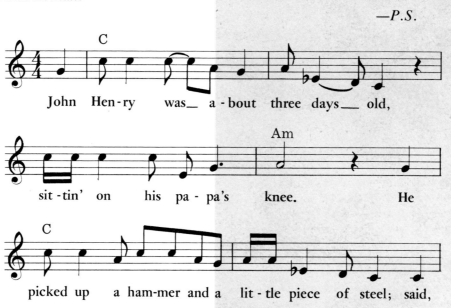

John Hen-ry was a-bout three days old, sit-tin' on his pa-pa's knee. He picked up a ham-mer and a lit-tle piece of steel; said,

32

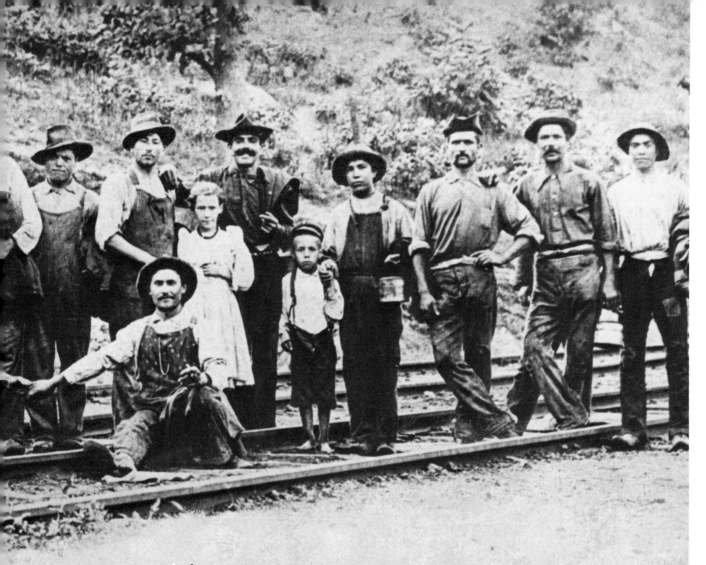

"Ham-mer's gon - na be the death of me, Lord, Lord.

Ham-mer's gon - na be the death of me."

(First line of final verse)

Well, ev - 'ry Mon - day__ morn - in' when the

blue - birds be - gin to sing_____

2. The captain said to John Henry
   "Gonna bring that steam drill 'round.
   Gonna bring that steam drill out on the job.
   Gonna whop that steel on down. Down,
     down.
   Whop that steel on down."

3. John Henry told his captain,
   "A man ain't nothin' but a man,
   But before I let your steam drill beat me
     down,
   I'd die with a hammer in my hand. Lord,
     Lord.
   I'd die with a hammer in my hand."

4. John Henry said to his shaker,*
   "Shaker, why don't you sing?
   I'm throwin' thirty pounds from my hips on
     down.
   Just listen to that cold steel ring. Lord, Lord.
   Listen to that cold steel ring."

5. The man that invented the steam drill
   Thought he was mighty fine,
   But John Henry made fifteen feet;
   The steam drill only made nine. Lord, Lord.
   The steam drill only made nine.

6. John Henry hammered in the mountain.
   His hammer was striking fire.
   But he worked so hard, he broke his poor
     heart.
   He laid down his hammer and he died. Lord,
     Lord.
   He laid down his hammer and he died.

7. John Henry had a little woman.
   Her name was Polly Ann.
   John Henry took sick and went to his bed.
   Polly Ann drove steel like a man. Lord,
     Lord.
   Polly Ann drove steel like a man.

* The "shaker" held and rotated the steel drill bit.

8. John Henry had a little baby.
   You could hold him in the palm of your
     hand.
   The last words I heard that poor boy say,
   "My daddy was a steel-driving man. Lord,
     Lord.
   My daddy was a steel-driving man."

9. Well, every Monday morning
   When the bluebirds begin to sing.
   You can hear John Henry a mile or more.
   You can hear John Henry's hammer ring.
     Lord, Lord.
   You can hear John Henry's hammer ring.

The Immigrants

"I can employ one half of the working class to kill the other half."
—Jay Gould

New people flooded this land from as far away as Ireland, Scandinavia, China.

Some employers used the low-paid immigrants to undercut existing wages, or to break strikes. When people blamed the newcomers, employers did little to discourage the growing hatred. Some even encouraged antagonism between ethnic groups. Prejudice was a good outlet for discontent among workers.

"They [the Irish] are nothing but imported beggars, animals . . . a mongrel mass of ignorance and crime and superstition, as utterly unfit for society's duties as they are for the common courtesies and decencies of civilized life."
—*Jersey City Standard*, 1859

• NO IRISH NEED APPLY •

Anonymous, 19th century

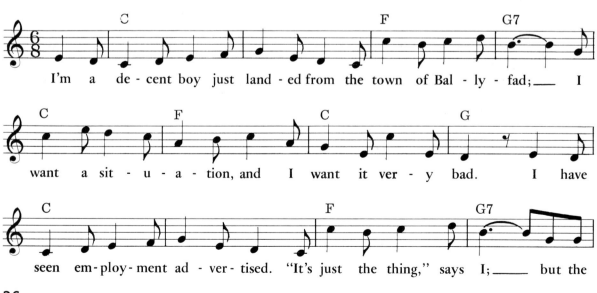

I'm a de-cent boy just land-ed from the town of Bal-ly-fad;— I
want a sit-u-a-tion, and I want it ver-y bad. I have
seen em-ploy-ment ad-ver-tised. "It's just the thing," says I;— but the

36

dirt - y spal - peen end - ed with "No I - rish need ap - ply." "Whoo," says

I, "that is an in - sult, but to get the place I'll try," So I

went to see the black-guard with his "No I - rish need ap - ply." Some do

think it a mis - for - tune to be chris - tened Pat or Dan, ___ But to

me it is an hon - or to be born an I - rish - man.

2. I started out to find the house; I got there
      mighty soon.
   I found the old chap seated; he was reading
      the *Tribune*.
   I told him what I came for, when he in a rage
      did fly.
   "No!" he says, "you are a Paddy, and no
      Irish need apply."
   Then I gets my dander rising, and I'd like to
      black his eye
   For to tell an Irish gentleman "No Irish
      Need Apply."

   REFRAIN

3. I couldn't stand it longer, so a-hold of him I
      took,
   And I gave him such a welting as he'd get at
      Donnybrook.
   He hollered "Milia Murther," and to get
      away did try,
   And swore he'd never write again "No Irish
      Need Apply."
   Well, he made a big apology. I bid him then
      goodbye,
   Saying, "When next you want a beating,
      write 'No Irish Need Apply.' "

   REFRAIN

The Field Slaves

In the same year that the Pilgrims landed at Plymouth Rock, a Dutch ship came to Jamestown with a cargo of African men and women—America's first slaves.

"Once the initial investment has been made, slaves are the most economical form of labor. We advise all who can afford to buy them to do so," said one South Carolina economist.

"The laboring class is unfitted for self government . . . master and slave is a relation as necessary as that of parent and child, and the northern states will yet have to introduce it."
—North Carolina newspaper, 1840s

"This is truly a PERFECT labor system."
—Unnamed supporter of slavery, circa 1850

• FOLLOW THE DRINKIN' GOURD •

Arranged by Paul Campbell

For most slaves, the only hope for freedom was escape. Once they were free, hundreds of the ex-slaves joined with abolitionists and sympathetic Northerners to set up an "Underground Railway," a trail of secret hiding places—barns, cellars, churches, and caverns—leading to the free North. Harriet Tubman, an escaped slave and "conductor" on the railway, went south nineteen times, risking her freedom and her life, to bring others out of slavery.

"I never run my train off the track, and I never lost a passenger."
—Harriet Tubman

Half a dozen times in this book we've given you a song which, though written in modern times, tells a story of the old days. This song was written by a fine young black composer in Boston in the 1970s.
—*P.S.*

• HARRIET TUBMAN •

by Walter Robinson

One night I dreamed I was in slav - 'ry.

'Bout eight-een fif - ty___ was the time.___ Sor - row___ was the
on - ly sign,___ noth-ing a - round___ to___ ease my mind.___
Out of the night___ ap-peared a la - dy lead-ing a dis - tant___
pil - grim band.___ "First mate,"___ she yelled, point-ing her hand,___
"make room on board___ for___ this young*wo - man,"Sing-ing, "Come on___ up –
I got a life - line; come on___ up to this train___ of mine.
Come on___ up – I got a life - line; come on___ up to this train___
___ of mine." She said her name was Har - ri - et Tub - man___ and she
drove for the un - der - ground___ rail - road.___

* Or "young man" or "old man," depending on the singer.

VERSE 3

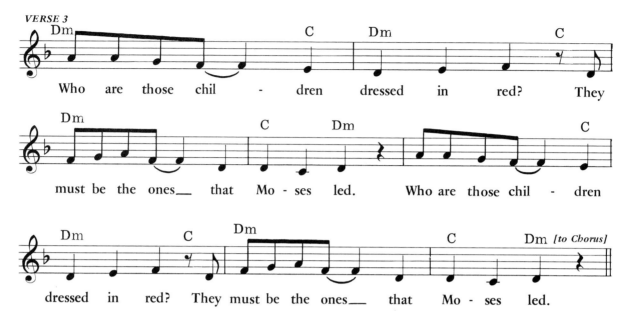

Who are those chil - dren dressed in red? They

must be the ones__ that Mo - ses led. Who are those chil - dren

dressed in red? They must be the ones__ that Mo - ses led.

2. Hundreds of miles we traveled onward
   Gathering slaves from town to town,
   Seeking every lost and found,
   Setting those free who once were bound.
   Somehow my heart was growing weaker;
   I fell by the wayside's sinking sand.
   Firmly did this lady stand,
   Lifted me up and took my hand, singing,
   CHORUS

3. Who are those children dressed in red?
   They must be the ones that Moses led.
   Who are those children dressed in red?
   They must be the ones that Moses led.
   CHORUS

"I looked at my hands to see if I was the same person, now that I was free. There was such a glory over everything. The sun come like gold through the trees and over the fields, and I felt like I was in heaven."

—Harriet Tubman

• OH, FREEDOM! •

Traditional

"Down the dusty road came ten miles of Negroes, bags packed for a journey longer than any man could understand, marching toward a future that could never again be built in the image of the past."
—Bruce Catton,
This Hallowed Ground

Oh, _____ free - dom!__ Oh, _____

free - dom!__ Oh, _____ free-dom o - ver

42

me. (o - ver me) And be - fore I'd be a

slave, I'd be bur - ied in my grave and go

home to my Lord and be free.

No more moaning. . .

No more weeping . . .

No more Jim-crow . .

There'll be singing . .

2

CHAPTER

EIGHT HOURS
1865–1900

"What do we want?
More schoolhouses and less jails
More books and less arsenals.
More learning, less crime.
More leisure, less greed.
More justice, less revenge."
—Samuel Gompers, circa 1898

During the Civil War, America's industry built up tremendous momentum. When the war ended, soldiers on both sides dropped their arms to take up tools to dig coal, build railways, cut timber, and do the thousands of other jobs that the expanding nation wanted.

"The Civil War unleashed the Demonic in American life," wrote historian Thomas Brooks. "Capital accumulated out of wartime profits searched for investments; the new trusts in oil, iron steel, copper, coal and coke rose as giants. . . ."

But prosperity was not shared by all. Though some, like Carnegie, Morgan, and Gould, amassed fortunes undreamed of before the war, the millions of people with laboring jobs remained, as Horace Greeley, the newspaper publisher, observed, "shamefully poor."

In 1873, the New York banking house of Jay Cooke & Company collapsed; the country went into an economic tailspin. Thousands of businesses closed. Three million people lost jobs. Only one out of five workers in America was left with steady work, usually with wages cut to less than a dollar a day.

The country had never seen such poverty.

"Here is a door. Listen! That short hacking cough, that helpless wail, what do they mean? The child is dying of measles. Here, in this tenement, number 59½, fourteen people died and eleven of them were children; in number 61, eleven, and eight of them not five years old. . . . Out in the alley itself, number 59, nine dead were carried out in 1882, five in baby coffins."
—Jacob Riis,
How the Other Half Lives

Those with money ignored the situation.

"I defy any man to show me that there is pauperism in the United States."
—Andrew Carnegie

"That you have property is proof of foresight on your part or if you have nothing is a judgment on your laziness or improvidence. . . . Too many are trying to live without labor . . . and too many squander their earnings on intoxicating drinks, cigars and amusements."
—Businessman, 1878

PERFECT BLISS !

Lured by promises of jobs, the flow of immigrants from China and Eastern and Central Europe grew to a torrent. When they arrived, the new settlers found whatever jobs they could—stripping and rolling cigars in their homes, peddling in the streets, or, if they were lucky, working in sweatshops from six in the morning till eight at night.

"Nearly any hour you can see them—pallid boy, spindly girl, their faces dulled, their backs bent under the heavy load of garments piled on head and shoulders. The boy always has bowlegs and walks with feet wide apart and wobbling. Here is a 'hoe man' in the making."
—*The New York Times*, 1881

"The clock in the workshop, it rests not a moment;
It points on, and ticks on; eternity—time;
Once someone told me the clock had a meaning,—
In pointing and ticking had reason and rhyme. . . .
At times when I listen, I hear the clock plainly;—
The reason of old—the old meaning is gone!
The maddening pendulum urges me forward
To labor and still labor on.
The tick of the clock is the boss in his anger.
The face of the clock has the eyes of the foe.
The clock—I shudder—dost hear how it calls me?
It calls me 'Machine' and it cries to me, 'Sew'!"
                    —Morris Rosenfeld,
                        sweatshop worker and poet, 1880

• MAYN YINGELE (MY LITTLE BOY) •

Words by Morris Rosenfeld
Translated by Aaron Kramer

Tune: Yiddish ballad, 1887

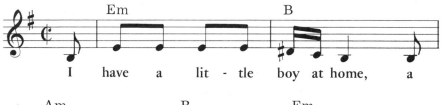

1. Ikh hob a kleynem yingele,
   A zunele gor fayn!
   Ven ikh derze im, dakht zikh mir,
   Di gantse velt iz mayn.

   Nor zeltn, zeltn ze ikh im,
   Mayn sheynem, ven er vakht,
   Ikh tref im imer shlofndik,
   Ikh ze im nor bay nakht.

2. Di arbet traybt mikh fri aroys,
   Un lozt mikh shpet tsurik;
   O, fremd iz mir mayn eygn layb,
   O, fremd mayn kinds a blik!

   Ikh kum tseklemterheyt aheym,
   In fintsternish gehilt—
   Mayn bleykhe froy dertseylt mir bald,
   Vi fayn dos kind zikh shpilt.

TRANSLATION:

I have a little boy, such a fine son! When I look at him, it seems to me that the whole world is mine. It's seldom though that I see my boy awake, for I always find him sleeping and see him only at night. My job drives me from home at dawn and lets me return only late, so that I hardly know my own child's looks.

My pale wife tells me how nicely the child plays, how sweetly he speaks, how cleverly he asks: "Oh, Mama, when will dear Papa come and bring me a penny?" I stand beside his little bed and hear him ask sleepily: "Oh where, oh where is my Papa?" I kiss the little blue eyes. They open, look at me and quickly close again. Depressed and embittered, I think to myself: One day, when you awake, my child, you will not find me anymore.

3. Vi zis es redt, vi klug es fregt:
   —O mame, gute ma,
   Ven kumt un brengt a peni mir,
   Mayn guter, guter pa?

   Ikh shtey bay zayn gelegerl
   Un ze, un her, un sha!
   A troym bavegt di lipelekh:
   —O, vu iz, vu iz pa?

4. Ikh kush di bloye eyegelekh;
   Zey efenen zikh—o, kind!
   Zey zeen mikh, zey zeen mikh
   Un shlisn zikh geshvind.

   Ikh blayb tseveytogt un tseklemt,
   Farbitert un ikh kler:
   Ven du dervakhst a mol, mayn kind,
   Gefinstu mikh nit mer . . .

An idea that had been germinating for years finally flowered.

"What must we workers do to combat the stranglehold of capital? We must unite ourselves into a Union of Unions. . . . Thus we will present a solid front to our enemies and cement our unity . . . throughout the nation."

—Labor newspaper, 1870s

• STEP BY STEP •

Words: anonymous

Tune: Traditional Irish

a cappella

Step by step the long - est march can be
won, can be won. Man-y stones can form an
arch, sing - ly none, sing - ly none. And by
un - ion what we will can＿ be ac-com - plished
still. Drops of wa - ter turn a
mill, sing - ly none, sing - ly none.

• HOLD THE FORT •

Words: anonymous, circa 1890s

Music by Philip Bliss, 1870

We meet to-day in free-dom's cause and

raise our voic-es high. We'll join our hands in

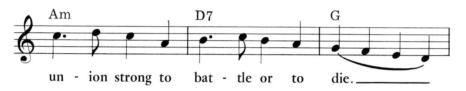

un-ion strong to bat-tle or to die.

CHORUS

Hold the fort, for we are com-ing,

Un-ion hearts be strong. Side by side we

bat-tle on-ward; vic-to-ry will come!

2. Look, my comrades, see the union
   Banners waving high,
   Reinforcements now appearing.
   Victory is nigh.
   CHORUS

3. See our numbers still increasing,
   Hear the buglers blow—
   By our union we shall triumph
   over every foe!
   CHORUS

4. Fierce and long the battle rages
   But we will not fear—
   Help will come whene'er it's needed.
   Cheer, my comrades, cheer!
   CHORUS

"An injury to one is the concern of all."

—creed of Knights of Labor

Two unions emerged, drawing working people from every part of the nation into their ranks—the Knights of Labor and the American Federation of Labor.

Originally a secret organization of working men, the Knights soon became a rallying place for "men and women of every craft, creed and color."

The American Federation of Labor opened its doors primarily to skilled workers who had already organized into smaller craft unions. Its goals were purposely simpler, geared to immediate issues of wages and hours.

"Mutual assistance among workers . . . solidarity among working people . . . universal brotherhood . . . education in reading and writing for working people . . . to secure for both sexes, equal pay for equal work . . . ."

• EIGHT HOURS •

Anonymous

We mean to make things o - ver. We are tired of toil for

naught, With but bare e-nough to live up - on And ne'er an hour for

thought.— We want to feel the sun - shine And we want to smell the

flowers. We are sure that God has willed it, And we mean to have eight

The unions had different objectives, but all agreed that the twelve-hour workday, dangerous working conditions, the near-starvation wages, the lack of education, the general degradation of life that had occurred in this new industrial age must end.

One issue especially became a call to action across the country, uniting all working men.

"... Eight hours shall constitute a legal day's labor from and after May 1, 1886."
—Proposition of the A.F.L., 1884

54

hours!__ We're sum-mon-ing our forc-es From the ship-yard, shop, and mill. Eight hours for work, eight hours for rest, Eight hours for what we____ will! Eight hours for work, eight hours for rest, Eight hours for what we will!____

CHORUS

On May 1, 1886, half a million workers across the country laid down their tools, vowing not to pick them up until they had won the eight-hour workday. It was America's most widespread strike. Men and women and children took to the streets and the parks with picnic baskets and parasols.

In Chicago the mood was different. As the *Tribune* said, "The railroads have stopped, the freight houses have closed, no smoke curls from the factory chimneys. It is like Sabbath." While eighty thousand workers and their families strolled down Michigan Avenue, Pinkerton detectives and city police lined the rooftops and National Guardsmen squatted behind machine guns. The stage was set for riot.

For three days the city waited. Then, on Monday, May 3, the tension broke.

Near the McCormick Harvesting Company on the South Side, police broke up a skirmish with clubs and guns, leaving four workmen dead. Outraged, the trade unionists planned to hold a protest meeting the next evening at Haymarket Square.

The next night it rained. Those who attended the meeting waited for hours for the speakers to arrive. By ten o'clock most of the small crowd had drifted away. Samuel Fielden, a preacher, was winding up a long rambling speech. Children were dozing on the laps of their mothers. Men were standing at the edge of the crowd, whispering among themselves, discussing how best to escape for a glass of beer.

"In conclusion . . ." Fielden was saying. Suddenly, he stopped. Standing behind the crowd was a column of 180 policemen.

"In the name of the State of Illinois, I command that this crowd immediately disperse!" a voice boomed. It was Police Captain John Bonfield, nicknamed "the clubber" by local people.

"But we are peaceable!" Fielden answered.

The police moved in.

There was a flash of red and an explosion. A dynamite bomb exploded on the ground between the crowd and the front ranks of the police. Dozens of people fell to the ground, wounded, killed. Without a moment's hesitation the police opened fire into the crowd.

"Suddenly it was chaos, the police firing in every direction, the people running in the darkness, trying to get away, trampling on one another, falling over dead bodies."

Before the smell of the bomb had even drifted away, seven policemen and fifteen crowd members lay dead on the pavement.

No one knew who had thrown the bomb. But that is not what the papers said. "Now it is blood!" they screamed. "The mob of Anarchists, crazed with a fanatic desire for blood, poured volley after volley into the police. Justice demands that these foreign assassins be tried for murder!"

The floodgates of hysteria opened wide. Even the staid *New York Times* shouted about "Anarchy's red hand!"

Under the urging of Chicago employers, local strike leaders were arrested and tried —not for murder, because there was no proof for that, but for "conspiracy." Despite the flimsiest evidence, seven men were sentenced to hang.

"These men are guilty of no crime," admitted one juror, "but they must hang. Organized labor will be crushed if they hang."

For the time being, the eight-hour-day movement was stopped. Workmen returned to their jobs and their twelve-hour workday with reduced salaries. The Knights of Labor, whose leaders attempted to disassociate themselves from the Haymarket debacle, ignominiously declined.

During the 1880s in Homestead, Pennsylvania, near Pittsburgh, Andrew Carnegie had built a great steel mill—the forerunner of the United States Steel Corporation.

"We go to work at seven in the morning and get through at night at six. We work that way for two weeks and then we work the long turn and change to the night shift of thirteen hours. The long turn is when we go on at seven Sunday morning and work through the whole twenty-four hours up to Monday morning. That puts us onto the night turn for the next two weeks, and the other crew onto the day."

—*Steelworker*, 1892

"One man jumps down, works desperately for a few minutes, and is then pulled up exhausted. Another immediately takes his place; there is no hesitation."

—Observer at a steel mill

When labor trouble erupted over work conditions, plant manager Henry Clay Frick tried to bring in three hundred strike breakers by river barge. These were Pinkertons, employees of the Pinkerton Detective Agency, whose specialty was helping employers stop strikes—by any means, including violence.

"At four o' clock in the morning a workers' patrol sighted the Pinkerton Barges a mile below Homestead. Whistles screamed through the town and ten thousand men,

58

women and children rushed down to the river bank. The barges hit the beach at dawn.''
　　　　—Milton Meltzer, *Bread and Roses*

The guards began to disembark. A gun went off. Pinkertons fired into the crowd.

''The women and children ran out of range. The men crouched behind the steel and pig iron stacked in the mill yard and returned fire. The Pinkertons took shelter in the barges. . . . When the guards finally ran up the white flag . . . three detectives and seven workers lay dead. . . . The Pinkertons were shipped back to Pittsburgh.''
　　　　—Thomas Brooks, *Toil and Trouble*

On July 12, Governor Patison of Pennsylvania sent in the state militia. At first the townspeople welcomed them, assuming that they were there to help. But they were under orders to take over the town and end the strike. Under martial law, the strike collapsed.

Carnegie, vacationing in Rome, wired his congratulations to Frick:

''LIFE WORTH LIVING AGAIN. . . . THE FIRST HAPPY MORNING SINCE JULY. . . . SURPRISING HOW PRETTY ITALIA. . . . HOMESTEAD—WE ARE ALL SICK OF THE NAME, BUT IT IS ALL OVER NOW. EVER YOUR PARD, A.C.''

Though nearly a hundred years old, this song is still sung in the bars around Homestead, Pennsylvania. The chorus needs some tenors to sing above the melody, as in the last line.

—*P.S.*

• THE HOMESTEAD STRIKE •

Words: Michael McGovern, "the puddler poet"   Tune: Traditional

We are ask - ing one an - oth - er,____ as we pass the time of day, Why work - ing-men re - sort to arms to get their prop-er pay, And why our la - bor un-ions____ should not be rec-og-nized,____ Whilst the ac - tions of a syn - di-cate____ must not be crit - i - cized.____ Now, the troub - les down at Home-stead____ were brought a - bout____ this way: When a grasp - ing cor - por - a - tion had the au - dac - i - ty to

61

say, "You must all re-nounce your un-ion___ and for-

swear your lib - er - ty And we will give you a

chance to live and die in slav - er - y."

CHORUS

Oh, the man that fights for hon - or, none can

blame him. May luck at-tend wher-

ev - er he may roam, (he may roam) And no

son of his will ev-er live to shame him, Whilst

lib-er-ty and hon-or rule our home.

2. When a group of sturdy workingmen
   started out at break of day,
   Determination in their face
   which plainly meant to say,
   "No one shall come and take our homes,
   for which we have toiled so long;
   No one shall come and take our place;
   no, it's here that we belong."
   A woman with a rifle
   spied her husband in the crowd.
   She handed him the weapon,
   and they cheered her long and loud.
   He kissed her and said, "Mary,
   you stay home until we're through."
   She said, "No, when there is trouble,
   my place is here with you."
   CHORUS

3. When a bunch of bum detectives came
   without authority,
   Like thieves at night, while decent men
   were sleeping peacefully,
   Can you wonder why all honest hearts
   with indignation burn,
   Or why the worm that treads the ground,
   when trod upon, will turn?
   When they locked out men at Homestead,
   then they were face to face
   With a grasping corporation,
   and they knew it was their place
   To protect their homes and families,
   and this was neatly done,
   And the public will reward them
   for the victories they won.
   CHORUS

In 1892, the miners of Coal Creek, Tennessee, walked out rather than sign an "ironclad" contract which would have prevented them from ever joining a union. The Tennessee Coal and Iron company retaliated by bringing in convict labor. Three times the miners entered the prisoner stockade and released the convicts. Three times, the state sent in the militia and brought the prisoners back. Finally, to make sure that the state would never send convicts again, the miners burned the stockade to the ground.

• ROLL DOWN THE LINE •

As sung by Uncle Dave Macon

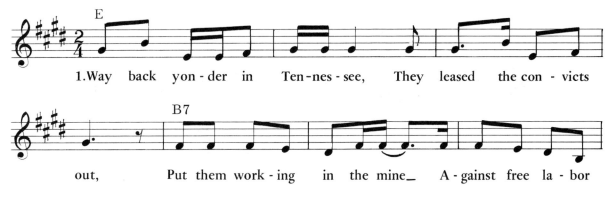

1.Way back yon-der in Ten-nes-see, They leased the con-victs out, Put them work-ing in the mine— A-gainst free la-bor

E

stout. Free la-bor re-belled a - gainst it. To win it took some

B7   E

time,   but while the lease was   in ef-fect, They made 'em rise and shine.

CHORUS

Bud-dy, won't you roll down   the   line? Bud-dy, won't you roll down   the

64

2. Early Monday morning
   They get you up on time,
   Send you down to Lone Rock
   Just to look into that mine;
       Send you down to Lone Rock
       Just to look into that hole,
       Very next thing the captain says:
       "You better get your pole."
           CHORUS

3. The beans they are half done,
   The bread is not so well;
   The meat it is all burnt up
   And the coffee's black as heck!
       But when you get your task done,
       And it's on the floor you fall,
       Anything you get to eat
       It 'ud taste good, done or raw.
           CHORUS

4. The boss, he is a hard man,
   A man you all know well;
   And if you don't get your task done
   He's gonna give you hallelujah!
       Carry you to the stockade,
       And it's on the floor you fall,
       Very next word you hear:
       "You better get your pole."
           CHORUS

line? Yon-der comes my dar-lin', com-ing down the line. Bud-dy, won't you roll down the line? Bud-dy, won't you roll down the line? Yon-der comes my dar-lin', com-ing down the line.

• A.R.U. •

Anonymous
Collected by Carl Sandburg

Been on the hum - mer since nine - ty - four.

Last job I had was on the Lake Shore.

Lost my of - fice in the A. R. U., And I

won't get it back till nine - teen - two.

And I'm still on the hog train flag - ging my meals,

Rid - in' the brake beams close to the wheels.

In 1894 Pullman workers joined the railroads' first industry-wide union—The American Railway Union. When the Pullman Company refused to deal with them, 125,000 A.R.U. members across the country walked out. The railroads had never seen such an effective strike. "We can handle the railway brotherhoods, but we cannot handle the A.R.U. . . . We have to wipe them out." They sent in scabs; they persuaded President Grover Cleveland to send in troops; and using political influence, they had the courts declare the strike illegal. Seven hundred strike leaders were arrested. The union's founder, Eugene V. Debs, was thrown into jail. The A.R.U. was finished, the strikers were blacklisted, and wound up "on the hog"—riding hog and cattle cars.

"We are born in a Pullman house, fed from the Pullman shop, taught in the Pullman school, catechized in the Pullman church, and when we die we shall be buried in the Pullman cemetery and go to the Pullman hell."
—Pullman worker

In 1893, the economy collapsed again. It was the worst depression of the century. Within a year almost four million people had lost their jobs. A new face appeared on the landscape—the tramp, the hobo. By the middle of the decade, an estimated hundred thousand men had taken to the road, without work or hope of finding work.

"Say, Mate, have you ever seen the mills
Where the kids at the loom spit blood?
Have you been in the mines when the fire damp blew,
Have you shipped as a hand with a freighter's crew,
Or worked in a levee flood?"

—Bill Quirke, hobo writer

• HALLELUJAH I'M A BUM •

Words by Harry McClintock, I.W.W.   Tune: "Revive Us Again"

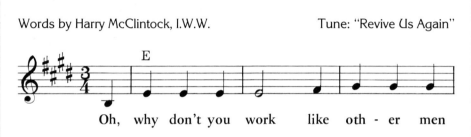

Oh, why don't you work like oth - er men

do? How the hell can I work when there's

B7   CHORUS   E

no work to do? Hal - le - lu - jah, I'm a

bum.   Hal - le - lu - jah, bum a -

B   E   3

gain.   Hal - le - lu - jah, give us a

C#m   B7   E

hand - out, to re - vive us a - gain.

2. Oh, I love my boss
   And my boss loves me,
   And that is the reason
   I'm so hungry.
   > CHORUS

3. Oh, the springtime has came
   And I'm just out of jail,
   Without any money,
   Without any bail.
   > CHORUS

4. I went to a house,
   And I knocked on the door;

A lady came out, says,
"You been here before."
   > CHORUS

5. I went to a house,
   And I asked for a piece of bread;
   A lady came out, says,
   "The baker is dead."
   > CHORUS

6. When springtime does come,
   Oh, won't we have fun—
   We'll throw up our jobs
   And we'll go on the bum.
   > CHORUS

• COXEY'S ARMY •

Words by Coxey's Army marchers   Tune: "John Brown's Body"

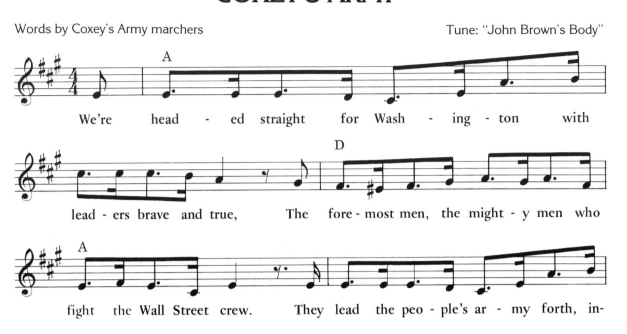

We're head - ed straight for Wash - ing - ton with

lead - ers brave and true, The fore - most men, the might - y men who

fight the **Wall Street** crew. They lead the peo - ple's ar - my forth, in-

"It was circus day when we came to town and every day was circus day, for there were many towns. We played the local nines with our baseball team; and we gave them better vaudeville than they'd often had, for there was good talent left in some of the decayed artists in the army."
—Jack London

jus - tice to un-do And truth goes march - ing

on. **CHORUS** Glo - ry, glo - ry Hal - le - lu - jah,

Glo - ry, glo - ry Hal - le - lu - jah, Glo - ry, glo - ry Hal - le -

lu - jah, And truth goes march - ing on.

As times grew worse, many turned to politics to solve their troubles. Believing that the Federal Government should provide jobs, Jacob Coxey, an Ohio businessman, organized an army of the unemployed to march on the Capitol: "a petition with boots on." They reached Washington, "marching silently and in good order. . . . Policemen were everywhere. . . . The army stopped. . . . Coxey, Brown and Jones walked alone toward the Capitol. The mounted police galloped after them. The leaders disappeared into the shrubbery; the police jumped their horses over and followed."
 —from *Coxey's Army* by Donald
 Le Crone McMurry

Coxey and his lieutenants were arrested for "trespassing on the grass." Coxey's "splendid mission" ended as a joke in newspapers across the country.

71

As unemployment lingered, a small Midwestern political party of farmers, working people, and small tradesmen exploded across the country: the Populist Party. Built on a platform of equality of sexes and races, direct election of senators, and control of big business, the little "People's" party swept the 1896 Democratic Convention and nominated William Jennings Bryan for President. Bryan lost to the business-backed McKinley by only half a million votes.

"Having behind us the producing masses of this nation and the world, supported by the commercial interests, the laboring interests, and the toilers everywhere, we will answer their [Republican] demand for a gold standard by saying to them: 'You shall not press down upon the brow of labor this crown of thorns. You shall not crucify mankind upon a cross of gold.' "
—William Jennings Bryan

• A HAYSEED LIKE ME •

Author unknown   Tune: "Acres of Clams"

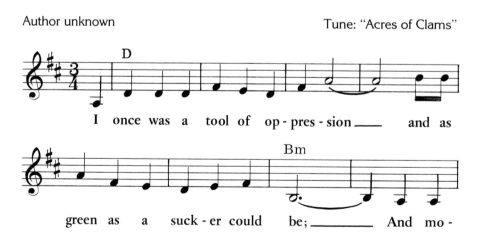

I once was a tool of op-pres-sion ___ and as

green as a suck-er could be; ___ And mo-

nop - o - lies band - ed to - geth - er_____ to break a poor hay - seed like me,_____ To break a poor hay - seed like me,_____ to break a poor hay - seed like me._____ Mo - nop - o - lies band - ed to - geth - er_____ to break a poor hay - seed like me._____

2. The railroads and old party bosses
   Together did sweetly agree
   They thought there would be little trouble
   In working a hayseed like me.

   In working a hayseed like me,
   In working a hayseed like me.
   They thought there would be little trouble
   In working a hayseed like me.

3. But now I have roused up a little;
   Their greed and corruption I see,
   And the ticket we vote next November
   Will be made up of hayseeds like me.

   Will be made up of hayseeds like me,
   Will be made up of hayseeds like me.
   And the ticket we vote next November
   Will be made up of hayseeds like me.

• FREE AMERICAY •

Author unknown   Tune: "The British Grenadiers"

We're brave and gal - lant min - er _ lads who _

work all un - der - ground   With

cour - age and good na - ture, none _

fin - er can_ be_ found. We_ work both late and

ear - ly, and get but lit - tle_

pay_____ To sup - port our wives and

chil - dren in_ Free A - mer - i - cay.

2. And when this strike is at an end
   and we have gained the day,
   We'll drink a health to our miner boys
   both near and far away.

Eight hours we'd have for working,
eight hours we'd have for play,
Eight hours we'd have for sleeping
in free Americay.

CHAPTER 3 SOLIDARITY FOREVER 1900–1918

America burst into the twentieth century with hope and confidence. New inventions "tumbled forth, one after the other: the sewing machine, the telegraph, refrigerated cars, typewriters, electric lights," creating new jobs and opportunities.

The price for this progress? The new immigrants paid with the lowest-paying jobs. Farmers paid much of it—crop failures and high shipping charges forced many to give up their land and become hired hands. Convicts paid—in many states indigents were

routinely thrown into chain gangs to provide cheap labor. Women in the mills huddled over machinery for twelve hours a day. Children crawled through mine shafts or worked in fields, dragging sacks of tobacco twice their size. With all the outward prosperity, America was still shamefully divided between the haves and the have-nots.

The Children

Though unions fought child labor, they were thwarted again and again, not only by manufacturers who needed the nimble fingers and cheap labor of children, but by workers themselves. Every time wages dropped, working families had to send their children to work to avoid starvation.

"They seem to be always cheerful and alert, taking pleasure in the light play of their muscles; enjoying the mobility natural to their age. . . . The work of these lively elves seemed to resemble a sport in which habit gave them a pleasing dexterity."
— Textile employer, circa 1900

"At five thirty in the morning, long lines of little gray children came out of the early dawn into the factories, into the madding noise, the lint filled rooms. Outside the birds sang. At lunch half-hour, the children would fall to sleep over their lunch of corn bread and fat pork. They would lie on the bare floor and sleep. Sleep was their only recreation, their release, as play is to a free child. . . . Often the little ones were afraid to go home alone at night. Then they would sleep on the floor."
— Autobiography of Mother Jones

"The golf links lie so near the mill
That almost every day
The laboring children can look out
And watch the men at play."
— Sara Norcliffe Cleghorn

• BABIES IN THE MILL •

by Dorsey Dixon

I used to be___ a fac - t'ry hand when things were mov - in' slow___ When chil - dren worked in cot - ton mills,___ each morn - in' had to go.___ Ev - 'r - y morn - in' just at five the

whis-tle___ blew on time_____ To get those ba - bies out of bed___ at the age of eight or nine._____ Get

CHORUS

out of bed_____ lit-tle sleep - y head and get your bite to eat._____ The fac - t'ry whis - tle's call - in' you;___ there's no more time to sleep.___

2. The children all grew up unlearned;
   they never went to school.
   They never learned to read or write;
   they learned to spin and spool.
   Every time I close my eyes
   I see before me still.
   What textile work was carried out
   by Babies in the Mill.
   CHORUS

3. Old-timer, can't you see that scene
   in the years gone by,
   When children worked in cotton mills
   the same as you and I?
   I know you're glad that times have changed
   and kids can have some fun.
   Now grown-ups go and do the work
   that babies used to run.
   CHORUS

"There was a crowd of about 200 men waiting there for a job. They looked hungry and kept watching the door. At last a special policeman came out and began pointing to the men, one by one. Each jumped forward. Twenty-three were taken. All the others turned their faces away and looked tired. I remember one boy sat down and cried, just next to me, on a pile of boards."

—Antonas Kaztaukis (pseudonym), from pages
of *The Independent,* 1906

• HE LIES IN THE AMERICAN LAND •

English lyrics adapted by Pete Seeger
from the original Slovakian

by Andrew Kovally
Pittsburgh, circa 1910
Transcribed by Jacob Evanson

1. Ah___ my God! What is this land of A-mer-i-ca?___

So___ man-y peo-ple trav-el-ing there.___

I will go___ too, for I am still young.

God, the Lord will grant me___ good luck there.

2. You, my wife, stay here till you hear from
    me.
   When you get my letter, put everything in
    order.
   Mount a raven-black steed, a horse like the
    wind.
   Fly across the ocean to join me here.

3. Ah, but when she arrived in this strange
    land,
   Here in McKeesport, this valley of fire,
   Only his blood, his grave did she find.
   Over it bitterly___she cried:

4. "Ah, ah, ah, my husband, what have you
    done to this family of yours?"
   "What can you say to these children, these
    children you've orphaned?"
   "Tell them, my wife, not to wait, not to wait,
    not to wait for me.
   "Tell them I lie *here*! In the American
    Land!"

The Farmers

"In addition to the higher prices that share-croppers had to pay for basics such as flour, meal, and sowbelly they were charged inter-est. . . . An interest rate of 40 percent annually was considered normal."
—H. L. Mitchell, *Mean Things Happening in This Land*

In the South, even Nature, in the form of a tiny bug, conspired to take away the sharecroppers' farms.

• THE BOLL WEEVIL •

Collected and Adapted by John and Alan Lomax

The boll wee-vil is a lit-tle black bug, from Mex-i-co they say, Come all the way to Tex-as,— Just a- look-in' for a place to stay. Just a-look-in' for a home,———— Just a-look-in' for a home.

6. Boll Weevil said to
   the merchant
   "I'll swing right on
   yo' gate;
   When I git through
   with yo' cotton,
   You'll sell that
   Cadillac Eight!"
   CHORUS

7. Boll Weevil said to
   the Doctor,
   "Better put away
   your pills;
   When I git through
   with the Farmer,
   Cain't pay no
   Doctor bills!"
   CHORUS

2. The Farmer said to the Boll Weevil,
   "I see you on the square."
   "Yes, sir," said the Boll Weevil,
   "My whole damn family's there!"
   CHORUS

3. The Farmer said to the Merchant,
   "I want some meat and meal."
   "Get outta here, you son-of-a-gun;
   Got Boll Weevil in yo' field!"
   CHORUS

4. The Farmer said to the Finance Man,
   "I'd like to make out a note."
   "Go to hell, you rascal you;
   Gotta Boll Weevil on yo' coat!"
   CHORUS

5. The Farmer said to the Banker,
   "I'd like to cash this check."
   "Get outta here you clodhopper;
   Gotta Boll Weevil down yo' neck!"
   CHORUS

8. Boll Weevil said to the Preacher,
   "Better close up them church doors;
   When I git through with the Farmer,
   Cain't pay no Preacher no more!"
   CHORUS

9. Boll Weevil said to the Business Man,
   "Boy, drink that cool lemonade.
   When I git through with you, boy,
   Gonna drag you outta that shade!"
   CHORUS

10. Boll Weevil in yo' field, boy,
    It's just like shooting dice,
    Work the whole damn year round,
    But the cotton won't bring no price!
    CHORUS

11. The Boll Weevil knocked on my front door;
    He said, "I've come to eat.
    I'm gonna starve you plumb to death
    And get the shoes right off yo' feet!"
    CHORUS

The Convicts Paid Also

"The supplying of convicts to plantation owners, construction contractors, and mine owners was so profitable a business that innocent men, many of whom were Negroes, were railroaded to jail to furnish convict labor to employers."

—Philip S. Foner, *History of the Labor Movement in the United States*

• TAKE THIS HAMMER •

Traditional
Adapted and arranged by John and Alan Lomax

Take_ this ham - mer (WAH!),* car - ry it to the cap - tain (WAH!); Take_ this ham - mer (WAH!), and car - ry it to the cap - tain (WAH!); Take this ham - mer (WAH!), and car - ry it to the cap - tain___ (WAH!). You tell him I'm gone___ (WAH!), you tell him I'm gone (WAH!).

2. If he asks you was I
    runnin',
        (3 times)
    Tell him I was flyin',
    Tell him I was flyin'.

3. If he asks you was I
    laughin',
        (3 times)
    Tell him I was
    cryin',
    Tell him I was
    cryin'.

4. I don't want no
    cornbread and
    molasses,
        (3 times)
    Hurts my pride,
    Hurts my pride.

5. I don't want no cold
    iron shackles
        (3 times)
    Round my leg,
    Round my leg.

* An unspellable sound of breath expelled as the hammer
falls.

The Women

New York City, Saturday, 1911:
"Children were playing hide and seek among the old trees in Washington Square Park. Suddenly . . . the muffled sound of an explosion. Passersby saw dark smoke oozing from the Asch Building on Greene Street."
—M. B. Schnapper, *Pictorial History of American Labor*

"I could see smoke pouring from the eighth and ninth floors. That was where Triangle Shirtwaist had its rooms. The faces of young women pressed up against the windows—hundreds of screaming heads. At one window a young man helped a girl onto the sill and let her drop, as gently as if he were helping her into a street car. That's when I heard my first thud. He brought another girl to the window. She kissed him. Then he held her in space and dropped her. In a flash he was out the window himself. His coat fluttered upward. The air filled his trouser leg. His hat remained on all the way down. . . . The girls had no other way out. The management had locked all the doors to keep them from going to the bathroom. . . . Thud . . . Another thud. . . . The thuds of the falling bodies grew so loud I thought they'd be heard all over the city."
—Excerpted from *The New York Times*

"Sometimes in my haste, I get my finger caught. The needle goes right through it. I bind the finger up with a piece of cotton and go on working."
—Sewing-machine operator, New York City

• BALLAD OF THE TRIANGLE FIRE •

by Ruth Rubin

In the heart of New York Cit - y, near Wash - ing - ton Square,— In nine - teen e - lev - en, March winds were cold and bare. A fire broke out in a build - ing_____ ten stor - ies_ high, And a hun - dred and for - ty six young girls in those_ flames did die.

2. On the top floor of that building, ten stories in the air,
   These young girls were working in an old sweatshop there;
   They were sewing shirtwaists for a very low wage,
   So tired and pale and worn-out!
   They were at a tender age.

3. The sweatshop was a stuffy room with but a single door;
   The windows they were gray with dust from off that dirty floor;
   There were no comforts, no fresh air, no light to sew thereby,
   And the girls, they toiled from early morn till darkness filled the sky.

4. Then on that fateful day—dear God, most terrible of days!—
   When that fire broke out, it grew into a mighty blaze.
   In that firetrap way up there with but a single door,
   So many innocent working girls burned, to live no more!

5. A hundred thousand mourners, they followed those sad biers.
   The streets were filled with people weeping bitter tears.
   Poets, writers everywhere described that awful pyre,
   When those young girls were trapped to die in the Triangle Fire.

Strike in the Mines

A series of long strikes focused the nation's attention on the plight of ordinary people and ignited the conscience of government. Slowly overdue reforms came.

In Pennsylvania, coal business boomed, but the eleven-hour day, treacherous work conditions, and child labor continued.

"From the cramped position they have to assume, most of them become deformed and back bent like old men. . . . Sometimes a terrified shriek is heard, and a boy is mangled and torn in the machinery, or disappears in the chute to be picked out later, smothered and dead. . . . Clouds of coal dust are so thick they penetrate every portion of the boys' lungs."
—John Spargo, investigator, 1906

In 1902, 145,000 Pennsylvania miners—Hungarians, Poles, Irish, Italians, Lithuanians and Russians—left the pits, vowing to stay out till the companies recognized their union. The companies refused.

"The rights and interests of the laboring man will be protected and cared for—not by labor agitators, but by the Christian men to whom God in His infinite wisdom has given control of the property interests of the country."
—George Baer, president of the Philadelphia and Reading
Railroad (one of the largest coal operators)

After nearly a year, President Theodore Roosevelt told both sides: arbitrate. For the first time, the United States Government intervened not to smash a labor dispute, but to settle it.

• A MINER'S LIFE •

Traditional
Collected by George Korson

Adapted by Fred Hellerman, Lee Hays,
Ronnie Gilbert and Frank Hamilton

"The United Mine Workers had crossed the threshold. . . . Unionism in the coal fields had been transformed from a wraith to a reality. It could be maimed but no longer could it be smashed."

— Sidney Lens

"Suffer?! . . . They don't suffer! Why, they can't even speak English!!"

— George Baer, president,
  Philadelphia and Reading
  Railroad

2. You've been docked and docked, my boys,
   You've been loading two to one.
   What have you to show for working
   Since this mining has begun?
   Overalls, and cans for rockers,
   In your shanties sleep on rails.
   Keep your hand. . . .

3. In conclusion, bear in mem'ry—
   Keep the password in your mind—
   God provides for every nation
   When in union they combine.
   Stand like men, and linked together;
   Victory will yet prevail.
   Keep your hand. . . .

Strike at the Mills

Lawrence, Massachusetts, was a mill town. Of 86,000 people living in its borders, 32,000 worked for the mills. Immigrants came from Italy, Russia, Syria, and Lithuania to find a haven. But the ten-hour, $2 day (25 cents a day for children) made Lawrence their purgatory.

"Any man who pays more for labor than the lowest sum he can get men for is robbing his stockholders. If he can secure men for $6 and pays more, he is stealing from the company."

— Stockholder of American Woolen, told to the Rev. Harry Emerson Fosdick, 1911

When a state law shortened the work week to fifty-four hours for women and children, Lawrence firms cut wages too. This was the last straw. As Sidney Lens described it in his book *The Labor Wars:* "On the afternoon of January 11, 1912, pay envelopes were passed around in the Everett Cotton Mill. Polish weavers counted their money

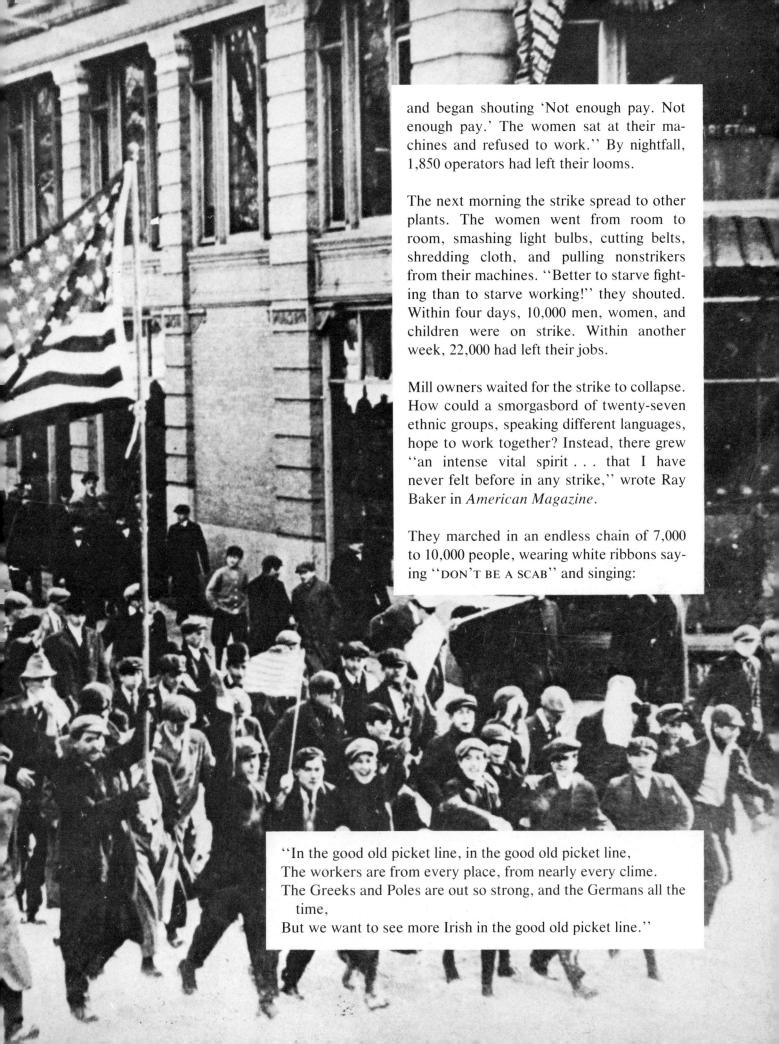

and began shouting 'Not enough pay. Not enough pay.' The women sat at their machines and refused to work.'' By nightfall, 1,850 operators had left their looms.

The next morning the strike spread to other plants. The women went from room to room, smashing light bulbs, cutting belts, shredding cloth, and pulling nonstrikers from their machines. ''Better to starve fighting than to starve working!'' they shouted. Within four days, 10,000 men, women, and children were on strike. Within another week, 22,000 had left their jobs.

Mill owners waited for the strike to collapse. How could a smorgasbord of twenty-seven ethnic groups, speaking different languages, hope to work together? Instead, there grew ''an intense vital spirit . . . that I have never felt before in any strike,'' wrote Ray Baker in *American Magazine*.

They marched in an endless chain of 7,000 to 10,000 people, wearing white ribbons saying ''DON'T BE A SCAB'' and singing:

''In the good old picket line, in the good old picket line,
The workers are from every place, from nearly every clime.
The Greeks and Poles are out so strong, and the Germans all the
    time,
But we want to see more Irish in the good old picket line.''

Families tried to send their children to safety in New York and Vermont. But something went wrong. "The children began to make their way to the train. The police, who had stationed themselves on both sides of the door, closed in on us with their clubs, beating left and right, with no thought of the children who were in danger of being trampled. The mothers and children both were hurled into a mass and bodily dragged to a military truck where they were clubbed again."
—Testimony, House Committee on Rules, 1912

The event, caught in photos by newsmen, so appalled the nation that the House Committee on Rules began a probe. A month later the mills agreed to negotiate.

With the strike over, employers tried to punish the leaders. As after the Haymarket affair thirty years before, strike leaders were charged with conspiracy. But times had changed. The jury of carpenters, barbers, sailmakers, grocers, and truck drivers found them not guilty.

"It is the first strike I ever saw that sang. I shall not forget the strange sudden fire of the mingled nationalities at the strike meetings when they broke into the universal language of song. Not only at the meetings did they sing, but at the soup houses and in the kitchens. I saw one group of women who were peeling potatoes at a relief station suddenly break into the swing of the 'Internationale.'"

—Ray Stannard Baker

Here's the famous old socialist song in every language in which it was sung on the square in Lawrence, Massachusetts. The original French still sounds best, we feel, and we urge you to try it that way. Don't slow it down. When songs get made official they are often slowed down to become more impressive. It's a mistake. To make a song official is worse than banning it. We present it in the original French, hoping you'll sing it in a brisk tempo. Get coaching on the pronunciation, if necessary. It's a good song. (Three of the original verses are omitted here.)

—*P.S.*

• L'INTERNATIONALE •

Words by Eugène Pottier, 1871   Music by Pierre Degeyter, 1888

Brisk march tempo

1. De - bout! les dam-nés de la ter - re! De -
bout! les for - çat; de la faim! La
rai - son tonne en son cra - tè - re: C'est l'é -
rup - tion de la fin. Du pas -
sé fai - sons ta - ble ra - se, Foule es -

clave, de - bout! de - bout! Le mon - de va chan - ger de

ba - se: Nous ne som - mes rien, so - yons

tout! C'est la lut - te fi -

na - le: Grou - pons - nous, et de - main, L'In -

ter - na - tio - na - le se - ra le genre hu -

main. C'est la lut - te fi - na - le: Grou - pons -

nous, et de - main, L'In - ter - na - tio -

na - le se - ra le genre hu - main.

2. Il n'est pas de sauveurs suprêmes:
   Ni Dieu, ni César, ni tribun,
   Producteurs, sauvons-nous nous-mêmes!
   Decrétons le salut commun!
       Pour que le voleur rende gorge,
       Pour tirez l'esprit du cachot,
       Soufflons nous-mêmes notre forge,
       Batton, le fer quand il est chaud!
           CHORUS

3. Ouvriers, paysans, nous sommes
   Le grand parti des travailleurs;
   La terre n'appartient qu'aux hommes,
   L'oisif ira loger ailleurs.
       Combien de nos chairs se repaissent!
       Mais si les corbeaux, les vautours,
       Un de ces matins, disparaissent,
       Le soleil brillera toujours!
           CHORUS

UNITED STATES

Arise, you prisoners of starvation!
Arise, you wretched of the earth!
For justice thunders condemnation.
A better world's in birth.
No more tradition's chains shall bind us.
Arise you slaves, no more in thrall!
The earth shall rise on new foundations.
We have been naught, we shall be all.
    'Tis the final conflict;
    Let each stand in his place.
    The international working class
    Shall be the human race.

ENGLAND

Arise! ye starvelings from your slumbers;
Arise ye criminals of want.
For reason in revolt now thunders,
And ends at last the age of cant.
Now away with all superstitions!
Servile masses, arise! arise!
We'll change forthwith the old conditions
And spurn the dust to win the prize.
    Then comrades, come rally,
    And the last fight let us face.
    The International
    Unites the human race.

SPANISH

Arriba, parias de la tierra!
En pie, famélica legión!

Los proletarios gritan: Guerra!
Guerra hasta el fin de la opresión
Borrad el rastro del pasado!
Arriba esclavos, todos en pié!
El mundo va a cambiar de base.
Los nada de hoy todo han de ser.
    Agrupémonos todos,
    En la lucha final.
    El género humano
    Es la Internacional.

ITALIAN

Compagni avanti il gran partito
Noi siamo dei lavorator.
Rosso un fiore in petto c'é fiorito.
Una fede c'é nata in cor.
Noi non siamo più nell'officina
Entro terra ai campi al mar
La plebe sempre all'opra china
Senza ideale in cui sperar.
    Su lottiamo! L'ideale
    Nostro alfine sará
    L'Internazionale
    Futura umanitá.

GERMAN

Wacht auf, Verdammte dieser Erde,
Die stets man noch zum Hungern zwingt!
Das Recht, wie Glut im Kraterherde,
Nun mit Macht zum Durchbruch dringt.
Reinen Tisch macht mit den Bedrängern!
Heer der Sklaven, wache auf!
Ein Nichts zu sein, tragt es nicht länger,
Alles zu werden, strömt zu Hauf!
    Völker, hört die Signale!
    Auf zum letzten Gefecht!
    Die Internationale
    Erkämpft das Menschenrecht!

DANISH

Rejs Jer! Fordomte her paa Jorden!
Rejs dig, du Sultens Slavehaer!
I Rettens Krater buldrer Torden,
nu er det sidste Udbrud maer!
Bryd kun Fortids more Mur i Stykker.
Slaveskarer, der er kaldt!
Snart Verdens Grundvold sig forrykker,
fra I ntet da vi bliver Alt!
    Vaagn til Kamp af jer Dvale,
    til den allersidste Dyst;
    —og Internationnale
    slaar Bro fra Kyst til Kyst.

SWEDISH

Upp trälar uti alla stater,
som hungern bojor lagt uppà.
Det dánar uti i rättens krater,
snart skall utbrottets timma slá.
Störtas skall det gamla snart i gruset
slav stig upp för att slá dig fri!
Frán mörkret stiga vi mot ljuset,
frán intet allt vi vilja bli.
 Upp till kamp emot kvalen.
 Sista striden det är,
 ty Internationalen
 ét alla lycka bär.

DUTCH

Ontwaakt, verworpenen der aarde
Ontwaakt, verdoemd' in hongersfeer
Reedlijk willen stroomt nu over d'aarde
En die stroom rijst al meer en meer
Sterft gij oude vormen en gedachten
Slaaf-geborenen ontwaakt, ontwaakt!
De wereld steunt op nieuwe krachten
Begeerte heeft ons aangeraakt.
 Makkers, ten laatsten male
 Tot den strijd ons geschaard
 En de internationale
 Zal morgen heerschen op aard'!

POLISH

Wyklęty powstań ludu ziemi.
Powstańcie, których dręczy głód.
Myśl nowa blaski promiennymi
Dziś wiedzie nas na bój, na trud.
Przeszlości ślad dłoń nasza zmiata,
Przed ciosem niechaj tyran drźy.
Ruszymy z posad bryle świata,
Dziś niczem, jutro wszystkiem my.
 Bój to będzíe ostatni,
 Krwawy skończy się trud,
 Gdy związek nasz bratni
 Ogarnie ludski ród.

RUSSIAN

Вставай, проклятьем заклейменный,
Весь мир голодных и рабов!
Кипит наш разум возмущенный
И в смертный бой вести готов.
Весь мир насилья мы разрушим
До основанья, а затем —
Мы наш, мы новый мир построим:
Кто был ничем, тот станет всем!
 Это есть наш последний
 И решительный бой.
 С Интернационалом
 Воспрянет род людской.

One striker carried a sign that read WE WANT BREAD AND WE WANT ROSES TOO. The words became an emblem for the strike.

"My ideas are what they are. They might be indicted, and you might believe that you can choke them; but . . . ideas can't be choked. . . . Do not believe that the cross or the gallows or the hangman's noose ever settled an idea."

—Joe Ettor, Lawrence strike leader

• BREAD & ROSES •

Words by James Oppenheim

Music by Mimi Fariña

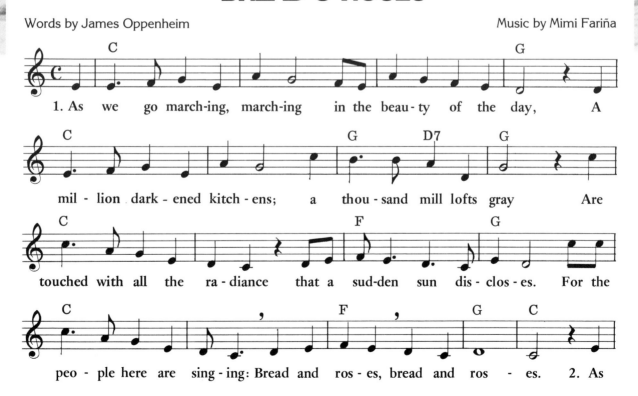

1. As we go march-ing, march-ing in the beau-ty of the day, A mil-lion dark-ened kitch-ens; a thou-sand mill lofts gray Are touched with all the ra-diance that a sud-den sun dis-clos-es. For the peo-ple here are sing-ing: Bread and ros-es, bread and ros-es. 2. As

we go march-ing, march-ing, we bat-tle too, for men. For they are in the

strug - gle, and to - geth - er we shall win. Our days shall not be

sweat - ed___ from_ birth un-til life clos - es. Hearts starve as well as

bod - ies: give us bread, but give us ros - es.___ 3. As

we go march - ing, march - ing, un - num - bered wom - en dead Go

cry - ing through our sing - ing their an-cient call for bread;___ Small

art and love and beau - ty their_ trudg - ing spir - its knew.___ Yes,

it is bread we fight for, but we___ fight for_ ros - es too. As

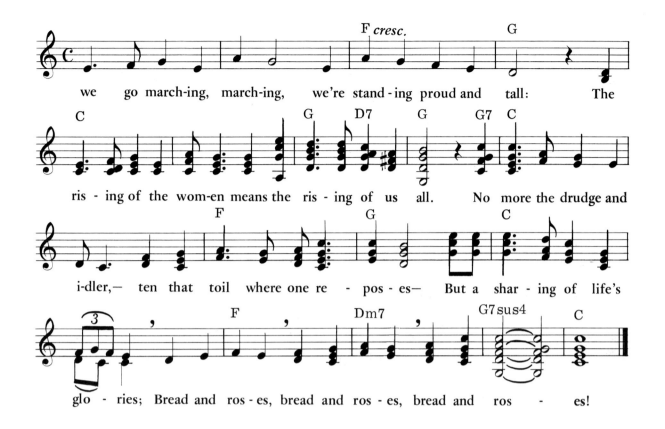

we go march-ing, march-ing, we're stand-ing proud and tall: The ris-ing of the wom-en means the ris-ing of us all. No more the drudge and i-dler,— ten that toil where one re-pos-es— But a shar-ing of life's glo-ries; Bread and ros-es, bread and ros-es, bread and ros-es!

This was an era of tragedy and an era of great ideals. Much about Lawrence—the participation of all ethnic groups and of women and children in major decisions, the democratic spirit—grew out of the philosophy of the union that organized the strike, the Industrial Workers of the World, or Wobblies. According to journalist Ray Stannard Baker, the I.W.W. sought "to bring together all workers in all industries. . . . They say that all workers should unite, just as capital is uniting."

They also had their share of detractors.

"We'll drive the goddamned sons-of-bitches into the river and drown them. We'll starve them. We'll kill every damned man of them or drive them, together with the Socialists, from the city!"
—Judge Davis, Minot, North Dakota, 1912

"MOVE ON" FOR SPEAKERS, LATER WILL INCLUDE PICKETS

• THE POPULAR WOBBLY •

Words by T-Bone Slim

Tune: "The Girls They Go Wild Simply Wild Over Me," by Fred Fisher

I'm as mild - man-nered man as can be,
And I've nev - er done them harm as I can see.
Still on me they put a ban, and they threw me in the can.
They go wild; simp - ly wild o - ver me.

2. They accuse me of rascality,
   But I can't see why they always pick on me.
   I'm as gentle as a lamb,
   But they take me for a ram;
   They go wild, simply wild over me.

3. Oh, the "bull" he went wild over me.
   And he held his gun where everyone could
       see.
   He was breathing rather hard
   When he saw my union card;
   He went wild, simply wild over me.

4. Then the judge he went wild over me,
   And I plainly saw we never could agree,
   So I let his nibbs obey
   What his conscience had to say;
   He went wild, simply wild over me.

5. Oh, the jailer he went wild over me,
   And he locked me up and threw away the
       key.
   It seems to be the rage,
   They like to keep me in a cage;
   They go wild, simply wild over me.

6. They go wild, simply wild over me.
   I'm referring to the bedbug and the flea;
   They disturb my slumber deep,
   And they rob me of my sleep;
   They go wild, simply wild over me.

7. Will the roses grow wild over me,
   When I'm gone into the land that is to be?
   When my soul and body part
   In the stillness of my heart,
   Will the roses grow wild over me?

WARNING PRIVATE PROPERTY KEEP OFF.

The "Blanket Stiff"

He built the ROAD—
With others of his CLASS, he built the road,
Now o'er it, many a weary mile, he packs his load,
Chasing a JOB. spurred on by HUNGERS goad.
He walks and walks, and wonders why
In H—L, he built the road.

The A.F.L. had done great things for skilled workers. But it was reluctant to deal with the millions of new industrial and migrant workers. However, the I.W.W. wanted to organize this "rabble." "We are going down into the gutter, to get at the mass of workers and bring them to a decent plane of living," said Big Bill Haywood, a founder of the I.W.W. Even hoboes were welcome. "Jesus Christ was a hobo" ran a Wobbly saying.

Many Wobblies became "jaw-smiths," or organizers, themselves. While working at their regular jobs they would hitchhike and boxcar-hop across the country, stopping off at factory towns and lumber camps, speaking and singing at the top of their lungs. They'd often stand across the street from the Salvation Army and preach their own sermon about "One Big Union for All."

Like the Salvation Army, the I.W.W. did much of its teaching through song. Joe Hill, a Swedish-American migrant worker who wrote songs between jobs, gave the Wobblies their own version of a favorite Salvation Army hymn, "The Sweet Bye and Bye."

• THE PREACHER AND THE SLAVE •

Words by Joe Hill   Tune: "The Sweet Bye and Bye"

1. Long-haired preach-ers come out ev-'ry night   Try to tell you what's wrong and what's right;   But when

104

asked, How 'bout some-thing to eat, They will
an-swer in voic-es so sweet: You will
eat, by and by, in that
glo-ri-ous land a-bove the sky. Work and
pray; live on hay. You'll get
pie in the sky when you die. *(That's a lie!)*

2. Oh, the Starvation Army they play
   And they sing and they clap and they pray,
   Till they get all your coin on the drum.
   Then they'll tell you when you're on the
       bum:

   CHORUS

3. If you fight hard for children and wife,
   Try to get something good in this life,
   You're a sinner and bad man, they tell;
   When you die you will sure go to Hell.

   CHORUS

4. Holy Rollers and Jumpers come out
   And they holler, they jump, and they shout.
   "Give your money to Jesus," they say;
   "He will cure all diseases today."

   CHORUS

5. Workingmen of all countries, unite.
   Side by side we for freedom will fight.
   When the world and its wealth we have
       gained,
   To the grafter we will sing this refrain:

   CHORUS

When the carmen of the Southern Pacific Railroad struck in 1911, Joe Hill taunted the scabbing engineers with a parody of a new pop song, "Casey Jones." The song was reprinted on little postcards, which were sold all over the country for a penny apiece to raise money for the strike.

"After God had finished the rattlesnake, the toad, the vampire, He had some awful substance left with which he made a scab. . . .

"A scab is a two-legged animal with a corkscrew soul, a water-logged brain, a combination backbone of jelly and glue . . . .

"When a scab comes down the street, men turn their backs, angels weep in heaven, and the Devil shuts the gates of Hell to keep him out. . . . Judas Iscariot was a gentleman compared to a scab. For betraying his master, he had character enough to hang himself. A scab has not."

—Jack London

"The strikebreaker is the hero of American industry."
—Charles W. Eliot, president of Harvard
University

• CASEY JONES •

Words by Joe Hill

Original tune adapted by T. Lawrence Seibert and Eddie Newton

The work-ers on the S. P. line to strike sent out a call;___ But Ca - sey Jones the en - gin-eer, he would-n't strike at all. His boil - er it was leak - ing, and its driv - ers on the bum, And his en - gine and its bear - ings, they were all out of plumb.

CHORUS
Ca - sey___ Jones kept his junk pile run-ning;__ Ca - sey___ Jones___ was work-ing dou - ble time. Ca - sey___ Jones got a wood-en med - al___ For be - ing good and faith - ful on the S. P. line.

2. The workers said to Casey, "Won't you help
    us win this strike?"
   But Casey said, "Let me alone; you'd better
    take a hike."
   Then Casey's wheezy engine ran right off the
    railroad track,
   And Casey hit the river with an awful smack.

   Casey Jones hit the river bottom;
   Casey Jones broke his blooming spine.
   Casey Jones became an angelino—
   He took a trip to heaven on the S.P. line.

3. When Casey got to heaven, up to the Pearly
    Gate,
   He said: "I'm Casey Jones, the guy that
    pulled the S.P. freight."
   "You're just the man," said Peter."Our
    musicians are on strike;
   You can get a job a-scabbing any time you
    like."

   Casey Jones got a job in heaven,
   Casey Jones was doing mighty fine.
   Casey Jones went scabbing on the angels
   Just like he did to workers on the S.P. line.

4. The angels got together and they said it
    wasn't fair
   For Casey Jones to go around a-scabbing
    everywhere.
   The Angels Union Number Twenty-three,
    they sure were there,
   And they promptly fired Casey down the
    Golden Stair.

   Casey Jones went to hell a-flying.
   "Casey Jones," the Devil said: "Oh, fine.
   Casey Jones, get busy shov'ling sulphur,
   That's what you get for scabbing on the
    S.P. line."

JOE HILL

"On November 19, 1915, Joe Hill, age 33, was shot by a five-man firing squad in the prison yard of the Utah State Penitentiary. Circumstantial evidence supported the allegation that he had shot and killed a Salt Lake City grocer. . . . His guilt is still a matter of dispute."

> —Joyce Kornbluth, *Rebel Voices,*
> University of Michigan Press,
> 1964

"Tomorrow I expect to take a trip to the planet Mars and, if so, will immediately commence to organize the Mars canal workers into the I.W.W. and we will sing the good old songs so loud that the learned stargazers will once and for all get positive proof that the planet Mars is really inhabited. . . . I have nothing to say for myself, only that I have always tried to make this earth a little bit better."

> —Joe Hill to editor Ben Williams,
> *Solidarity,* 1915

"My will is easy to decide
For there is nothing to divide
My kin don't need to fuss and moan
'Moss doesn't cling to a rolling stone.'

"My body?—Oh! if I could choose,
I would to ashes it reduce
And let the merry breezes blow
My dust to where some flowers grow.

"Perhaps some fading flower then
Would come to life and bloom again
This is my last and final will.
Good luck to all of you."

> —Joe Hill

110

• JOE HILL •

Words by Alfred Hayes

Music by Earl Robinson

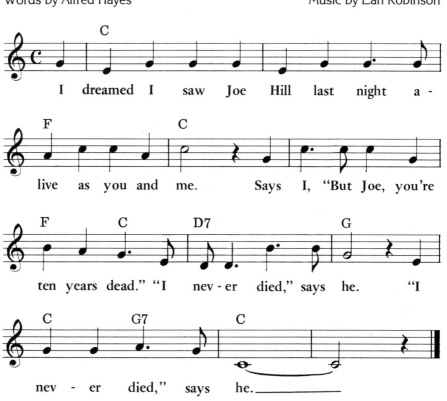

I dreamed I saw Joe Hill last night a-live as you and me. Says I, "But Joe, you're ten years dead." "I nev-er died," says he. "I nev-er died," says he._____

2. "In Salt Lake, Joe, by God," says I,
   Him standing by my bed,
   "They framed you on a murder charge."
   Says Joe, "But I ain't dead."
   Says Joe, "But I ain't dead."

3. "The copper bosses killed you, Joe.
   They shot you, Joe," says I.
   "Takes more than guns to kill a man,"
   Says Joe, "I didn't die."
   Says Joe, "I didn't die."

4. And standing there as big as life
   And smiling with his eyes,
   Joe says, "What they forgot to kill
   Went on to organize,
   Went on to organize."

5. "Joe Hill ain't dead," he says to me;
   "Joe Hill ain't never died.
   Where working men are out on strike,
   Joe Hill is at their side,
   Joe Hill is at their side."

6. "From San Diego up to Maine
   In every mine and mill
   Where workers strike and organize,"
   Says he, "you'll find Joe Hill";
   Says he, "you'll find Joe Hill."

7. I dreamed I saw Joe Hill last night
   Alive as you and me.
   Says I, "But Joe, you're ten years dead."
   "I never died," says he.
   "I never died," says he.

The First World War came along. In that era of superpatriotism and mistrust of foreigners, popular sentiment swung against the I.W.W. When the union took a strong antiwar stance, the Federal Government jailed its leaders for violation of the War Espionage Act and confiscated all records. The organization never recovered. However, the I.W.W.'s ideals, their songs, their faith in "one big union" survived to change the face of American Labor.

"When the . . Wobblies came, the sheriff says, 'Don't you come no further.
Who the hell's yer leader anyhow?
Who's yer leader!?'
And them Wobblies yelled right back,
'We don't have a leader.
WE'RE ALL LEADERS,'
And they kept right on comin'."
—Wobbly story from *Nevada Worker*, quoted by C. Wright Mills

• SOLIDARITY FOREVER •

Words by Ralph Chaplin

Tune: "John Brown's Body"

When the un - ion's in - spi - ra - tion through the work - ers' blood shall run, There can be no pow - er great - er an - y - where be-neath the sun, Yet what force on earth is weak - er than the fee - ble strength of one? But the un - ion makes us strong.

CHORUS

Sol - i - dar - i - ty for - ev - er! Sol - i - dar - i - ty for -

112

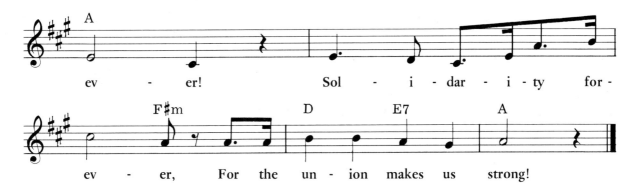

ev - er! Sol - i - dar - i - ty for-

ev - er, For the un - ion makes us strong!

2. They have taken untold millions that they
  never toiled to earn,
  But without our brain and muscle not a
  single wheel could turn.
  We can break their haughty power, gain our
  freedom when we learn
  That the union makes us strong.

3. In our hands is placed a power greater than
  their hoarded gold,
  Greater than the might of armies magnified a
  thousandfold.
  We can bring to birth a new world from the
  ashes of the old,
  For the union makes us strong.

MEMORIAL SERVICES HELD AT MT. PLEASANT CEMETERY FOR THE EVERETT VICTIMS MAY-1-1917

CHAPTER 4 TALKIN' UNION 1918–1945

"Years ago I recognized my kinship with all living things, and I made up my mind that I was not one bit better than the meanest on earth. I said then and I say now, that while there is a lower class I am in it, while there is a criminal element I am in it, and while there is a soul in prison, I am not free."

—Eugene V. Debs, founder American Railway Union

"The American businessman came out of the war ready to lick the next thing that stood in his way. Labor stood in his way. Mingling his [patriotic] with his selfish motives, he developed a fervent belief that 100 percent Americanism implied the right of the businessman to kick the union organizer out of his shop. . . . He was quite ready to believe that a struggle of American laboring men for better wages was the beginning of an armed struggle directed by Lenin."

—Frederick Lewis Allen, *Only Yesterday*

"Unions may have been justified in the past, but now there is no necessity for them . . . Their existence is inimical to the best interest of employees, employers, and the general public."

—President of U.S. Steel Corporation, circa 1920

114

"... Tool maker, stacker of wheat,
Player with railroads and the nation's freight handler
Stormy, husky, brawling,
City of the big shoulders."

—Carl Sandburg, *Chicago*

WE WANT THE WORLD WITH A PICKET FENCE AROUND IT, SEE?

DON'T BE AN UGLY DISSATISFIED WORKMAN. BE GLAD YOU HAVE A GOOD JOB AND WAGES TO KEEP YOURSELF AND FAMILY IN COMFORT.

"Working men don't need unions nowadays. . . . We are much more in danger of coddling the working men than abusing them."
—Unnamed business leader quoted in *Middletown* by Robert and Helen Lynd

This "American plan" found fertile ground in the anti-Red hysteria that swept the country following news of the Bolshevik Revolution in Russia. The wartime fervor now carried over into a domestic war against Communists, Socialists, labor organizers, and "free-thinkers of all kinds."

In 1920, a factory worker and a fish peddler, both active in labor causes, were dragged off a streetcar in West Bridgewater, Massachusetts, and booked for murder. Witnesses swore that Nicola Sacco and Bartolomeo Vanzetti had been nowhere near the scene of the crime. The prosecutor and judge didn't dispute this, but insisted that Sacco

116

and Vanzetti, though innocent of this particular crime, were "morally guilty because they are the enemies of our existing institutions."

A young attorney, Felix Frankfurter, the future Supreme Court justice, observed that "by exploitation of the defendants' alien blood, their imperfect knowledge of English, their unpopular social views, and their opposition to the war, the District Attorney invoked against them a riot of political passion and patriotic sentiment. . . ."

After a seven-week trial the jury found them guilty. The sentence was death.

Political leaders and unions like the International Ladies' Garment Workers' Union, the United Mine Workers, the New York Furriers, and the Colorado miners demonstrated and petitioned for a retrial. But in 1927, Sacco and Vanzetti went to the electric chair.

"If it had not been for these thing, I might have live out my life talking at street corners to scorning men. I might have die unmarked, unknown, a failure. Now we are not a failure. . . . Never in our full life could we hope to do such work for tolerance, for justice, for man's understanding of man as now we do by accident."
—Bartolomeo Vanzetti, 1927

• TWO GOOD ARMS •

by Charlie King

Who will re-mem-ber_ the hands so white and fine_ That touched the fin-est lin-en,_ that poured the fin-est wine?_

Who will re-mem-ber_ the gen-teel words they spoke_ To name the lives of two_ good_ men— a nui-sance or a joke?_

CHORUS

All who know_ these_ two good arms_ know I'd nev-er had to rob or kill. I can live by my own two_ hands and live well, And all my life I have strug-gled_ To rid the earth of all such crime.

* Use a C chord in the last verse.

2. Who will remember Judge Webster Thayer,
   One hand on the gavel, the other resting on
      his chair?
   Who will remember the hateful words he
      said,
   Speaking to the living in the language of the
      dead?

CHORUS

3. Who will remember the hand upon the
      switch
   That took the lives of two good men in the
      service of the rich?
   Who will remember the one that gave the
      nod
   Or the chaplain standing near at hand to
      invoke the name of God?

CHORUS

4. We will remember this good shoemaker,
   We will remember this poor fish peddler,
   We will remember all the strong arms and
      hands
   That never once found justice in the hands
      that rule this land.

FINAL CHORUS

And all who knew these two good men
Knew they never had to rob or kill.
Each had lived by his own two hands,
And they lived well.
And all their lives they had struggled
To rid the earth of all such crime.
And all our lives we must struggle
To rid the earth of all such crime.

Black Workers

During the economic boom that had begun in 1915, more than a million blacks moved north to work in the war industries. But after the war, when the soldiers returned, the black workers suddenly found themselves with no jobs. Moreover, most were not even allowed to join unions. For many the only job available was strikebreaker. The only place most could live was in urban black "ghettos."

"My grandfather was born in Georgia. When he got free, he and my grandma moved to Alabama and started one-mule tenant farming. They called the mule 'Bailey.' Only, by the second winter they were so close to starving, they ate him. . . . They moved on. . . . They were still moving years later when I was born. In Lexington, my uncle Ned got himself arrested. We never did find out the charge. They put him in shackles with a ball and chain and made him a slave again. . . .

"So we moved . . . and we moved . . . and we moved. . . . When I was old enough, I got myself a job in a railroad shop at thirty cents an hour, seven days a week. But the white man next to me was getting a dollar twenty-five an hour. I mentioned this to the foreman. Of course you know what he said: "If you don't like it, move."
                                    —Hosea Hudson

• BLACK, BROWN, AND WHITE BLUES •

by William (Big Bill) Broonzy

Just lis-ten to this song I'm sing-ing, broth-er;

You'll know it's true.

If you're black and got to work for a liv-ing, boy,

This is what they'll do: Now, if you're white, you're

right. And if you're brown, stick a-

round, But if you're black, oh, broth-er,

Git back, git back, git back.

I was in a place one night
They was all having fun.
They was all drinking beer and wine,
But me, I couldn't buy none.
CHORUS

I was in an employment office;
I got a number and stood in line.
They called everybody's number
But they never did call mine.
CHORUS

Me and a man's working side by side.
This is what it meant;
He was getting a dollar an hour,
I was making fifty cents.
CHORUS

I helped build this country;
I fought for it too.
Now . . . I want to know
What you gonna do about the Jim Crow.
CHORUS

121

New scientific management theories grew up, calculating precisely the optimum use of machinery—including workers.

"Usually, the employer picks the fastest girl in the place and does a time study on her. When she turns out more than the average worker, that becomes the new amount expected and the price per piece is cut accordingly. . . . We have to work faster and faster just in order to make the same amount."
—Testimony before Senate
Committee on Manufacturing
1926

122

• HURRY, HURRY, HURRY •

Circa 1925; author unknown

Tune: "John Brown's Body"

Mine eyes have seen the glo - ries of the mak-ing of ___ a Ford. It's
made un - der con - di - tions that would of - fend e - ven the Lord. With a
most un - god - ly hur - ry and a - midst a wild up - roar, Pro -
duc - tion rush - es on. Hur - ry, hur - ry, hur - ry, hur - ry!
Hur - ry, hur - ry, hur - ry, hur - ry! Hur - ry, hur - ry, hur - ry,
hur - ry! Pro - duc - tion rush - es on.

(slow tempo again)

2. Be quick, my soul, to answer, and be quicker still, my feet;
Be fifty diff'rent places ev'ry time my heart doth beat.

The whip that drives me onward is my family must eat!

(pick up tempo)
Production rushes on.
CHORUS
(faster and faster)

123

But as factories became more efficient, unemployment climbed and wages dropped. Purchasing power shriveled. In October of 1929, the wheels of industry just stopped.

When the stock market crashed, there were two million unemployed in America. Within a year, more than four million were out of work. Economic experts kept predicting that the Depression would end, that employment would climb. But by 1933, the number of unemployed had jumped to fifteen million.

Many of industry's "captains" refused to believe what was happening.

"Never before has American business been as firmly entrenched for prosperity. . . . Just grin and keep on working."
—Charles M. Schwab, president
of Bethlehem Steel

"We are now past the worst. . . . With continued unity of purpose, we shall recover."
—President Herbert Hoover, 1930

127

• RAGGEDY, RAGGEDY ARE WE •

Words by John Handcox;
last verse by Lee Hays

Tune: "How Beautiful Heaven Would Be"

Rag - g'dy, rag - g'dy are we, Just as rag-g'dy as rag - ged-y can be. We___ don't get noth-ing for our la - bor, so rag - g'dy, rag - g'dy are we.

* F is a helluva key for the guitar, isn't it? Put this in any key you like—P.S.

2. So hungry, hungry are we,
Just as hungry as hungry can be.
We don't get nothing for our labor,
So hungry, hungry are we.

3. So homeless, homeless are we,
Just as homeless as homeless can be.
We don't get nothing for our labor,
So homeless, homeless are we.

4. So landless, landless are we,
Just as landless as landless can be.
We don't get nothing for our labor,
So landless, landless are we.

5. So cowless, cowless are we,
Just as cowless as cowless can be.
The planters don't 'low us to raise 'em,
So cowless, cowless are we.

6. So hogless, hogless are we,
Just as hogless as hogless can be.
The planters don't 'low us to raise 'em,
So hogless, hogless are we.

7. So cornless, cornless are we,
Just as cornless as cornless can be.
The planters don't 'low us to raise it,
So cornless, cornless are we.

8. Union, union are we,
Just as union as union can be.
We're gonna get something for our labor,
For union, union are we.

"I am opposed to any government dole," said President Hoover. Official subsidization of idleness "is an abhorrent notion . . . local relief should be kept as distasteful as possible to avoid encouraging shiftlessness."

"In Oregon I saw thousands of bushels of apples rotting in the orchards. . . . When I left Seattle, I saw women searching for scraps of food in the refuse piles."
—Testimony, Congressional investigation, 1932

• THE SOUP SONG •

Words by Maurice Sugar   Tune: "My Bonnie Lies Over the Ocean"

2. I spent twenty years in the fact'ry;
   I did everything I was told.
   They said I was loyal and faithful,
   Now, even before I get old:

3. I saved fifteen bucks with my banker,
   To buy me a car and a yacht.
   I went down to draw out my fortune,
   And this is the answer I got:

4. I fought in the war for my country.
   I went out to bleed and to die;
   I thought that my country would help me,
   But this was my country's reply:

5. I fell on my knees to my Maker;
   I prayed every night to the Lord.
   I swore to be faithful forever,
   And now I've received my reward.

In Harlan County, Kentucky, eleven thousand miners walked out protesting a 10-percent wage cut. The National Guard arrested strike leaders and escorted scabs into the mines. A week later, Sheriff J. H. Blair raided the homes of union officers and charged them with first-degree murder. That night, the wife of one union leader put her fury into the words of "Which Side Are You On?"

• WHICH SIDE ARE YOU ON? •

Words by Florence Reece

Music: traditional

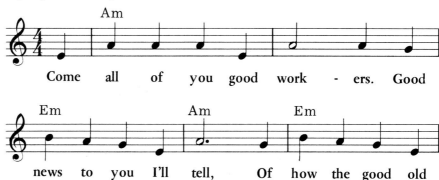

"We are six brothers, all six feet tall. Our shoulders are lurched forward, as if trying to fend off a blow. When we walk, our arms dangle down most to the knee. We are not as good looking as we used to be. We mine coal . . . we burrow, like a wild animal, clawing its hole for hibernation. . . . Our days are lived in the dark, bent in a strained crouch, our heads set well back between the shoulders, necks bent like a goose-necked hoe. . . . Our eyes curve upward as if we study the weather, but we look for the treacherous "horsebacks," slate that drops without warning and leaves a hole the size of a horse's back, crushing whatever it falls on. We are always looking up. . . . But this is America! We are part of her! Our fathers were dangerous men. They took guns and went bare-footed with Washington. There may come a time when we are dangerous men. . . . Must our children follow our stumbling feet!? . . Our kids, they're all that matter now."
—*United Mine Workers Journal,* 1931

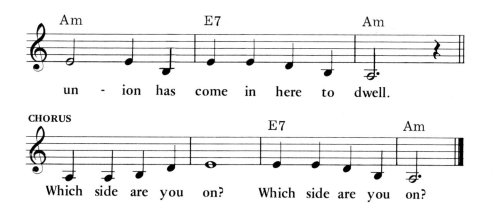

un - ion has come in here to dwell.

CHORUS

Which side are you on? Which side are you on?

2. Don't scab for the bosses,
   Don't listen to their lies.
   Us poor folks haven't got a chance
   Unless we organize.
   CHORUS

3. They say in Harlan County
   There are no neutrals there.
   You'll either be a union man
   Or a thug for J.H. Blair.
   CHORUS

![Photograph of women standing behind a wooden fence with a sign reading "THE GOVERNOR SENDS AID TO PIXLEY 24 DEPUTY SHERIFFS 11 HIGHWAY PATROLMEN WE WANT FOOD!"]

4. Oh, workers can you stand it?
Oh, tell me how you can.
Will you be a lousy scab,
Or will you be a man?
CHORUS

5. My daddy was a miner,
And I'm a miner's son;
And I'll stick with the union
Till every battle's won.
CHORUS

*This is the original last verse
as sung by Mrs. Reece's
two daughters:*

My daddy is a miner,
He's in the air and sun,*
But he'll stick with the union
Till every battle's won.

* Blacklisted.

In 1932, fifteen thousand World War I veterans marched into Washington, dressed in uniform, under the glorious-sounding name of the "Bonus Expeditionary Force." They had come to collect bonuses which the government had promised them in 1919.

"They are truck drivers and blacksmiths, steelworkers and coalminers, stenographers and common laborers. They are black and white. Some talk fluently of their woes, some can muster only enough English to tell you where they came from and why. . . . But, they nearly all have one thing in common—a sense of the futility of individual struggle, a consciousness of being in the grip of cruel incomprehensible forces."
—Thomas Henry, *The
(Washington) Evening Star*

They set up a makeshift camp on the Mall in front of the Capitol and waited for those in power to take notice. President Hoover finally noticed. With tear gas, with torches, "with four companies of infantry, four troops of cavalry, a machine gun squadron, and six whippet tanks," said Irving Bernstein in *The Lean Years,* the Army burned them out. . . . Two veterans and an eleven-week-old baby were killed.

"Thank God we still have a government that knows how to deal with a mob."

—Herbert Hoover

• BEANS, BACON, AND GRAVY •

Author unknown

Tune: "Ballad of Jesse James"

During the First War, when Hoover was food commissioner, they used to say, "Eat every bean and pea on the plate."

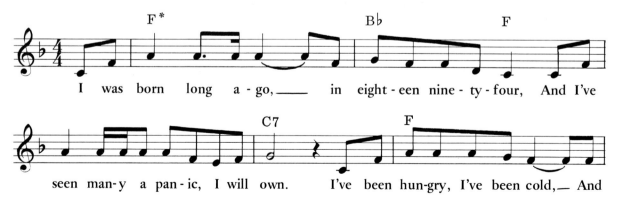

I was born long a-go,—— in eight-een nine-ty-four, And I've
seen man-y a pan-ic, I will own. I've been hun-gry, I've been cold,— And

* Again, play this in any key you like.

now I'm grow-ing old, But the worst I've seen is nine-teen thir-ty - one.

CHORUS

Oh, those beans, ba-con, and grav-y,— They al-most drive me cra-zy.— I

eat them till I see them in my dreams *(in my dreams).* When I

wake up in the morn-ing—— and an-oth-er day is dawn-ing, Yes, I

know I'll have an-oth-er mess of beans.

2. We congregate each morning
   At the country barn at dawning,
   And everyone is happy, so it seems.
   But when our work is done,
   We file in one by one
   And thank the Lord for one more mess of
     beans.

   CHORUS

3. We have Hooverized on butter,
   For milk we've only water,
   And I haven't seen a steak in many a day.
   As for pies, cakes, and jellies,

We substitute sowbellies,
For which we work the country road each
  day.

CHORUS

4. If there ever comes a time
   When I have more than a dime,
   They will have to put me under lock and key,
   For I've been broke so long
   I can only sing this song
   Of the workers and their misery.

   CHORUS

Hoover was out. Franklin Roosevelt became President. For the first time in years, the government would actively support the unions.

"I pledge you, I pledge myself, a new deal for the American people."
—Franklin D. Roosevelt

Many employers bitterly refused to give up the power over labor they had exercised for so many years. They fought the unions with tear gas . . .

with scabs . . .

with company-paid spies, like the notorious "Chowderhead" Cohen, "266 pounds of stool pigeon."

"And please don't let them sit down in my factory"

• I DON'T WANT YOUR MILLIONS, MISTER •

Words by Jim Garland

Tune: traditional

I don't want your mil-lions, mis-ter,____ I don't want____ your dia-mond ring;____ All I want____ is the right to live, mis-ter.____ Give me back____ my job a-gain.____

2. I don't want your Rolls-Royce, mister;
   I don't want your pleasure yacht;
   All I want is food for my babies;
   Give to me my old job back.

3. I know you have a land deed, mister;
   The money is all in your name;
   But where's the work that you did, mister?
   I'm demanding back my job again.

4. We worked to build this country, mister,
   While you enjoyed a life of ease;
   You've stolen all that we built, mister;
   Now our children starve and freeze.

5. Think me dumb if you wish, mister;
   Call me green or blue or red;
   This one thing I sure know, mister:
   My hungry children must be fed.

6. I don't want your millions, mister,
   I don't want your diamond ring.
   All I want is the right to live, mister.
   Give me back my job a-gain.

When North Carolina textile workers struck against sweatshop conditions and seventy-two-hour weeks, employers called in state troopers. Fourteen workers were killed. But this was not the 1920s. The mill workers fought back with fury.

"The only place that could be secured for the meeting was the front of a dilapidated Negro schoolhouse. . . . On the steps stood a mixed group of whites and Negroes and their wives, singing out their story and their hopes. . . . On the road above, a group of State 'Po-lice' and guards watched, their guns conspicuously displayed."
—Helen Norton Starr, as quoted in *Songs of Work & Protest*

• WE SHALL NOT BE MOVED •

Words by textile workers

Tune: "I Shall Not Be Moved"

CHORUS

We shall not, we shall not be moved.

We shall not, we shall not be moved. Just like a

141

tree that's plant - ed by the wa - ter,_____
we___ shall not___ be moved._____

VERSE

The un - ion is be - hind us (we shall not be moved);__ the
un - ion is be - hind us (we shall not be moved). Just like a
tree that's plant - ed by the wa - ter,
we_____ shall not__ be__ moved._____

2. We're fighting for our freedom . . .

3. We're fighting for our children . . .

4. We'll build a mighty union . . .

5. ———is our leader . . .

New verses composed in the 1980s:

6. We are young and old together . . .

7. We are black and white together . . .

8. We are city and country together . . .

9. We are women and men together . . .

In 1935, John L. Lewis, the president of the United Mine Workers, joined with the heads of a dozen other industrial unions to form the Committee for Industrial Organization. Instead of the relatively small craft unions which had existed until then, Lewis envisioned large industry-wide unions, powerful enough to stand up to huge corporations. They would represent the tens of millions of industrial workers, women workers, and black workers still outside the labor movement.

Renamed the Congress of Industrial Organizations, the C.I.O. grew with the strength of an avalanche.

"If I went to work in a factory the first thing I'd do would be TO JOIN A UNION"

Franklin D Roosevelt

CIO RESEARCH AND EDUCATION DEPARTMENT

"For the first time in history, a drive to organize the millions of unskilled workers in basic industry was to get under way, backed by established organizations with millions of dollars and adequate experience. When the zeal of youth and the ardor of a mass crusade were added to the experience and money, the combination was to prove irresistible."

—Richard Boyer and Herbert Morais, *Labor's Untold Story,* United Electrical, Radio, and Machine Workers, 1970

"Millions of C.I.O buttons sprouted on overalls, shirtwaists, and workers' caps. They became badges of a new independence."

—Edward Levinson

"Heed this cry that comes from the hearts of men. Organize the Unorganized."

—John L. Lewis, 1935

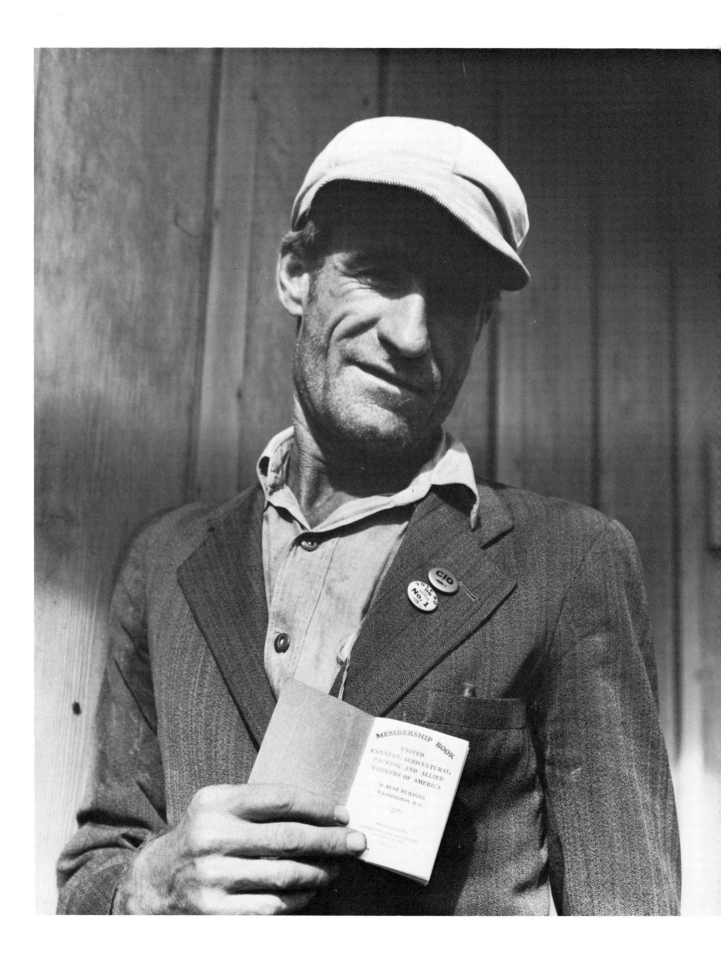

This song almost wrote itself. I and the other Almanac Singers were singing mainly for C.I.O. unions in 1941, and one day Mill Lampell paraphrased a verse of the old "Talking Blues": "If you want to go to heaven/ Let me tell you what to do." Within a few hours, Lee and Mill had two-thirds of the song written. The only trouble was we couldn't see how to end it. A couple of weeks later, mulling it over, I realized there was no solution except in the old slogan "Stick together." So, ignoring the rhyme, I slung on the last two stanzas, and we had a song.

—P.S.

• TALKING UNION •

by Millard Lampell,
Lee Hays and Pete Seeger

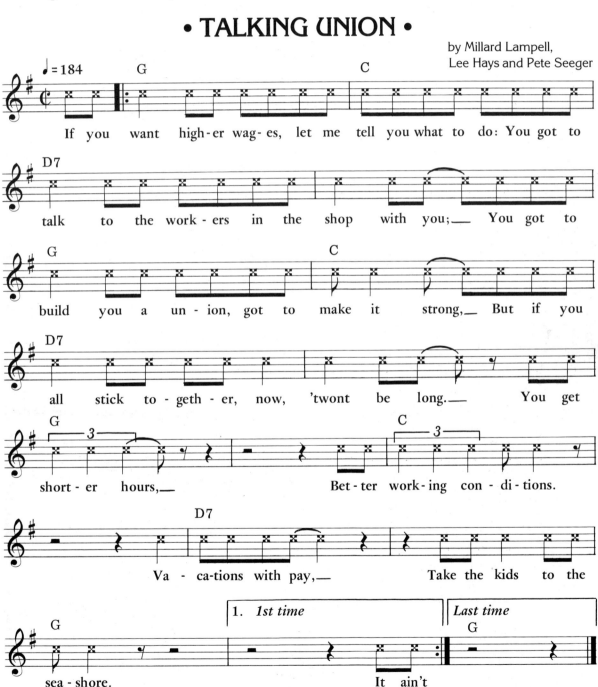

2. It ain't quite this simple, so I better explain
   Just why you got to ride on the union train;
   'Cause if you wait for the boss to raise your pay,
   We'll all be waiting till Judgment Day;
   We'll all be buried—gone to Heaven—
   Saint Peter'll be the straw boss then, folks.

3. Now, you know you're underpaid, but the boss says you ain't;
   He speeds up the work till you're about to faint.
   You may be down and out, but you ain't beaten,
   You can pass out a leaflet and call a meetin'—
   Talk it over—speak your mind—
   Decide to do something about it.

4. 'Course, the boss may persuade some poor damn fool
   To go to your meeting and act like a stool;
   But you can always tell a stool, though—that's a fact;
   He's got a rotten streak a-running down his back;
   He doesn't have to stool—he'll make a good living
   On what he takes out of blind men's cups.

5. You got a union now, and you're sitting pretty;
   Put some people on the steering committee.
   The boss won't listen when just one squawks,
   But he's got to listen when the union talks.
   He better—he'll be mighty lonely.

6. Suppose they're working you so hard it's just outrageous,
   And they're paying you all starvation wages:
   You go to the boss, and the boss would yell,
   "Before I raise your pay I'd see you all in hell."
   Well, he's puffing a big cigar and feeling mighty slick,
   He thinks he's got your union licked.
   He looks out the window, and what does he see
   But a thousand pickets, and they all agree
   He's a bastard—unfair—slave driver—
   Bet he beats his wife.

7. Now, folks, you've come to the hardest time:
   The boss will try to bust your picket line.
   He'll call out the police, the National Guard;
   They'll tell you it's a crime to have a union card.
   They'll raid your meeting, hit you on the head.
   Call every one of you a doggone Red—
   Unpatriotic—Moscow agents—bomb throwers, even the kids.

8. But out in Detroit here's what they found,
   And out in Frisco here's what they found,
   And out in Pittsburgh here's what they found,
   And down at Bethlehem here's what they found:

   That if you don't let Red-baiting break you up,
   If you don't let stool pigeons break you up,
   If you don't let vigilantes break you up,
   And if you don't let race hatred break you up—
   You'll win. What I mean, take it easy—but take it.

146

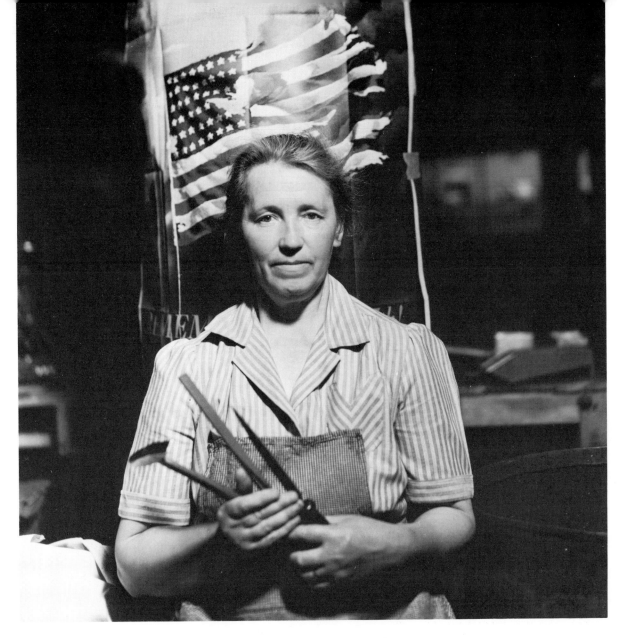

• I AM A UNION WOMAN •

by Aunt Molly Jackson

Freely, Kentucky Mountain Style

I am ___ a un - ion wom-an, ___ just as brave ___ as I can be. I

do not___ like___ the boss-es,___ and the
boss-es don't like me.

CHORUS

Join___ the C. I. O. Come
join___ the C. I. O.

2. I was raised in old Kentucky,
   In Kentucky borned and bred,
   But when I joined the union,
   They called me a Rooshian Red.
   CHORUS

3. This is the worst time on earth
   That I have ever saw,
   To get killed out by gun thugs,
   And framed up by the law.
   CHORUS

4. When my husband asked the boss for a job,
   This is the words he said:
   "Bill Jackson, I can't work you, sir;
   Your wife's a Rooshian Red."
   CHORUS

5. If you want to join a union,
   As strong as one can be,
   Join the dear old C.I.O.,
   And come along with me.
   CHORUS

6. We are many thousand strong,
   And I am glad to say
   We are getting stronger
   And stronger ev'ry day.
   CHORUS

7. If you want to get your freedom,
   Also your liberty,
   Join the dear old C.I.O.,
   Also the I.L.D.*
   CHORUS

8. The bosses ride big fine horses
   While we walk in the mud,
   Their banner is the dollar sign,
   And ours is striped with blood.
   CHORUS

* International Labor Defense

In the auto industry, workers were paid by the piece. When the company wanted to raise production, it speeded up the machines and dropped the price for each piece produced. Employees had to work harder just to keep from losing salary.

It was not only the hated "speedup" that made them strike at Fisher Auto Body—it was the heat and bad air as well. According to newspaper accounts, during a heat wave in 1936, dozens of workers died, hundreds collapsed. In Michigan's auto cities, the ambulance did not stop wailing for more than a week.

"You should see my husband come home at night . . . so tired like he was dead . . . at night in bed he shakes, his whole body, he shakes . . . " "They're not men any more if you know what I mean. They're not men. My husband he's only thirty but to look at him you'd think he was fifty and all played out."

—Auto workers' wives quoted in
The Labor Wars by Sidney Lens

Around Christmas of 1936, the company cut the piecework price again. "To hell with this stalling!" someone shouted. Someone else turned off the power in the plant. The lights went out. The machines stopped. For a moment, the workers looked at one another, not sure what to do next. Most went home. A thousand decided to stay—this would be a "sit-down strike."

"The men divided themselves into families of fifteen, each finding its own nook to set up house. Sleeping facilities were either car cushion wadding or the insides of unfinished car bodies, lovingly called 'Mill Hotel' or 'Hotel Astor.' Every man had to put in six hours a day, in the kitchen, on patrol duty, or cleaning up. . . . Each evening before the daily meeting, there was an hour of singing and entertainment, most of it provided by sympathetic artists outside."

—Sidney Lens, *The Labor Wars*

The company tried to evict them. In subfreezing temperatures, it shut off the heat. Company guards blocked the doors, making it impossible for food to get into the plant. The women tried to raise a ladder outside, but the guards grabbed it from them. They called in the police. Squad cars squealed into the parking lot, and fifty policemen ran toward the building hurling tear gas. The wind, however, which was on the side of the strikers, blew it back into their faces.

"Pickets to your posts. Men, get your fire hoses going!" shouted Victor Reuther, one of the strike leaders. The strikers hauled out two huge hoses, aimed them at the police, and let go. Soaking wet and freezing, the police retreated. Several policemen pulled out their guns. A shot exploded. "I've been hit!" shouted one striker. Then everyone joined in. The women outside the plant ran at the police, screaming and turning over cars. More hoses came from the plant windows, dousing the attackers.

By midnight, the police were gone. Forever in union lore this would be known as "The Battle of Bulls Run"—the night when the bulls ran.

"When we finally pulled the switch and there was quiet, I remembered something, that I was a human being, that I could stop those machines, that I was better than those machines anytime."

—Striker, 1936

149

• SIT DOWN •

by Maurice Sugar

When they tie the can to a un - ion man, Sit

down!— Sit down! When they give him the sack, They'll—

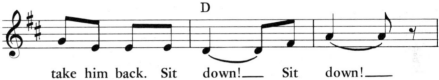

take him back. Sit down!— Sit down!—

CHORUS

Sit down; just take a seat. Sit down, and rest your feet.

Sit down; you've got 'em beat. Sit down! Sit down!

2. When they smile and say, "No raise in pay,"
Sit down! Sit down!
When you want the boss to come across,
Sit down! Sit down!
    CHORUS

3. When the speedup comes, just twiddle your thumbs.
Sit down! Sit down!
When you want 'em to know they'd better go slow,
Sit down! Sit down!
    CHORUS

4. When the boss won't talk, don't take a walk.
Sit down! Sit down!
When the boss sees that, he'll want a little chat.
Sit down! Sit down!
    CHORUS

151

"They said, 'We're going in!' We said, 'Over our dead bodies!' Then they started to charge. Within seconds all of us were there. Down the street—women, children, old people! Row after row. We were singing. That's when we found out we were a union!"
—Member, United Automobile Workers
Women's Auxiliary

• UNION MAID •

Words by Woody Guthrie

Tune: "Pretty Redwing"

There once was a un-ion maid Who nev-er was a-fraid Of
goons and ginks and com-pa-ny finks or dep-u-ty sher-iffs who
made the raid. She went to the un-ion hall When a meet-ing it was
called, And when the com-pa-ny boys came 'round She al-ways stood her
ground. Oh, you can't scare me. I'm stick-in' to the un-ion,___
___ I'm stick-in' to the un-ion,___ I'm stick-in' to the un-ion.___
___ Oh, you can't scare me. I'm stick-in' to the un-ion;___
___ I'm stick-in' to the un-ion___ till the day I die.___

2. This union maid was wise
   To the tricks of the company spies.
   She'd never be fooled by the com-
      pany stools;
   She'd always organize the guys.
   She'd always get her way
   When she struck for higher pay.
   She'd show her card to the company guard,
   And this is what she'd say:
   CHORUS

For history's sake:
   When the union boys they seen
   This pretty little union queen
   Stand up and sing in the deputies' face,
   They laughed and yelled all over the place.
   And you know what they done,
   These two-gun company thugs?
   When they heard this union song
   They tucked their tails and run.
   CHORUS

A new verse for the 1980s:
   You women who want to be free,
   Just take a little tip from me:
   Break out o' that mold we've all been sold;
   You got a fightin' history.
   The fight for women's rights
   With workers must unite
   Like Mother Jones, bestir them bones
   To the front of every fight.
   CHORUS

* I wish I could remember who wrote this one!—P.S.

Out West, Depression farmers were fighting another enemy: dust.

On Armistice Day 1933, a blizzard moved out of the Great Plains, burying Chicago and moving eastward. A day later, it blanketed Buffalo and Albany in snow. But no snow like this had ever fallen before: it was black as soot, because it carried the topsoil of a thousand farms. For the next four years, one windstorm after another would blow across the plains states, tearing the thin topsoil from the farms and turning them into useless sand dunes.

"By mid morning a gale was blowing, cold and black. . . . There was a wall of dirt one's eyes could not penetrate, but it could penetrate the eyes and ears and nose. It could penetrate to the lungs until one coughed up black. If a person was outside, he tied his handkerchief around his face, but he still coughed up black. . . . When the wind died and the sun shone forth again, it was on a different world. There were no fields, only sand drifting into mounds. . . . There was no longer a road. In the farmyard, fences, machinery and trees were gone, buried. The roofs of sheds stuck out through drifts deeper than a man is tall."
—R. D. Lusk, *The Life and Death of 470 Acres*

"Just sitting here, counting the Kansas farms blowing by."
—Kansas farmer watching a "duster"

"This actually happened in Pampa, Gray County, Texas, April 14, 1935. I was there. The storm was as black as tar and as big as an ocean. It looked like we was done for. Thousands of us packed up and lit out."
—Woody Guthrie

155

• SO LONG! IT'S BEEN GOOD TO KNOW YOU •

by Woody Guthrie

CHORUS

2. The dust storm hit, and it hit like thunder.
   It dusted us over, it dusted us under,
   It blocked out the traffic, it blocked out the
     sun,
   And straight for home all the people did run,
     singing:
     CHORUS

3. We talked of the end of the world, and then
   We'd sing a song and then sing it again.
   We'd set for an hour and not say a word,
   And then these words would be heard:
     CHORUS

4. The sweethearts set in the dark and they
     sparked,
   They hugged and kissed in that dusty old
     dark,
   They sighed and cried, they hugged and they
     kissed,
   But instead of marriage, they was talkin' like
     this:
     CHORUS

5. The telephone rang, and it jumped off the
     wall,
   And that was the preacher a-making his call.
   He said, ''Kind friend, this may be the end;
   You got your last chance at salvation from
     sin.'' Well,
     OMIT CHORUS

6. The churches was jammed, the churches was
     packed;
   That dusty old dust storm blowed so black,
   The preacher could not read a word of his
     text.
   He folded his specs, took up collection, said:
     CHORUS

7. This was the dustiest dust storm that blowed,
   And most everybody they took to the road.
   They lit down the highway as fast as could
     go,
   And sung this song as they blowed:
     CHORUS

The farmers abandoned their exhausted farms to the banks and the crows, and joined a huge migratory river of evicted sharecroppers and tenant farmers, out-of-work industrial workers, and hoboes, all moving west, looking for work.

"They came through US Highway 30, through the Idaho hills, along Highway 66 along the Old Spanish Trail through El Paso, along all the other Westward trails. They came in decrepit, square shouldered 1925 Dodges and 1927 La Salles; in battered 1923 Model T Fords; in trucks piled high with mattresses and cooking utensils and children, with suitcases and jugs and sacks strapped to the running boards."
—Frederick Lewis Allen, *Only Yesterday*

Woody kept to a strict tempo in this song, but was always adding or subtracting beats at unexpected places. No two verses come out alike.

• PASTURES OF PLENTY •

by Woody Guthrie

Free meter

It's a might - y hard row that my poor hands has hoed._____ My poor feet has trav - eled a hot dust - y road.___ _____ Out of your Dust___ Bowl and west - ward we rolled, and your des - erts was hot and your moun-tains_____ was cold. _____

2. I worked in your orchards of peaches and prunes;
   Slept on the ground in the light of the moon.
   On the edge of the city, you'll see us, and then
   We come with the dust and we're gone with the wind.

3. California, Arizona, I make all your crops.
   Then it's north up to Oregon to gather your hops,
   Dig the beets from your ground, cut the grapes from your vine
   To set on your table your light, sparkling wine.

4. Green pastures of plenty from dry desert ground,
   From the Grand Coulee Dam where the waters run down,
   Every state in the union us migrants has been.
   We'll work in this fight, and we'll fight till we win.

5. It's always we rambled, that river and I;
   All along your green valley I will work till I die.
   My land I'll defend with my life if it be,
   'Cause my pastures of plenty must always be free.

Out West they found that the agricultural valleys of California and Oregon had been bought up by large combines and banks. If the farmers wanted work, they would have to get in line with Mexican and Japanese migrant workers and pick apples or grapes for 50 cents a day.

For the first time in their lives, the farmers began to "talk union."

"These farmers . . . will fight for their rights at the drop of a hat . . . they will be dangerous people. They will fight for what they want."

—Social worker, quoted in *You Have Seen Their Faces* by Erskine Caldwell

They were reflecting a new spirit in America, a growing conviction that the country was not just for the rich, for the successful, for the industrialists and their families; it belonged to everyone.

"We manage to get along."

—Tenant farmer's wife

• THIS LAND IS YOUR LAND •

by Woody Guthrie

CHORUS

This land is your land,____ this land is my land,

from Cal - i - for - nia____ to the New York is - land,

From the red - wood for - est____ to the Gulf Stream wa - ters;____

____ This land was made for you and me.____

Fine

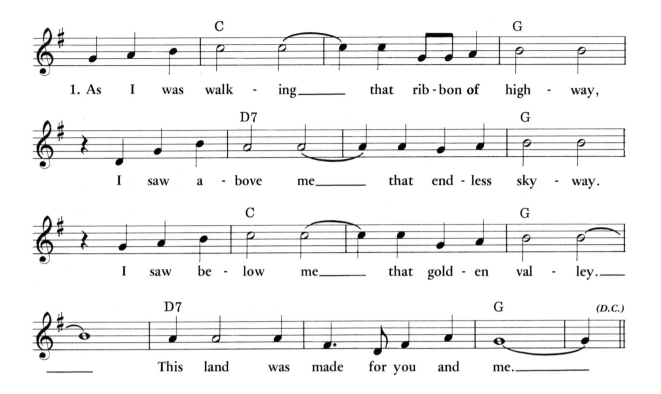

1. As I was walk-ing____ that rib-bon of high-way,
I saw a-bove me____ that end-less sky-way.
I saw be-low me____ that gold-en val-ley.____
____ This land was made for you and me.____

2. I roamed and rambled,
   and I followed my footsteps
   To the sparkling sands of
   her diamond desert,
   While all around me
   a voice was chanting:
   "This land was made for you and me."
   CHORUS

3. In the squares of the city
   by the shadow of a steeple,
   By the relief office
   I saw my people.
   As they stood there hungry,
   I stood there whistling
   (what was he whistling?):
   "This land was made for you and me."
   CHORUS

4. Was a great high wall there
   that tried to stop me;
   Was a great big sign there

   says "Private Prop'ty."
   But on the other side
   it didn't say nothin'—
   That side was made for you and me.
   CHORUS

5. Nobody living
   can ever stop me,
   As I go walking
   that freedom highway.
   Nobody living
   can make me turn back.
   This land was made for you and me.
   CHORUS

6. The sun was shining
   as I was strolling
   And the wheat fields waving
   and the dust clouds rolling.
   As the fog was lifting,
   a voice was chanting:
   "This land was made for you and me."
   CHORUS

162

"What's good for General Motors is good for America."
—Charles Erwin Wilson, president, General Motors Corporation

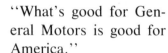

Ten million troops came home from World War II. Five years of fighting had ended. Now they could reap the fruits of peace.

"We seek . . . more than an end to war, we want an end to the beginning of all wars. . . . The only limit to our realization of tomorrow will be our doubts of today."
—Franklin D. Roosevelt, written the night before his death

"Lord God . . .
Measure out new liberties so none shall suffer for his father's color or credo of his choice:
Post proofs that Brotherhood is not so wild a dream as those who profit by postponing it pretend:
Sit at the treaty table and convey the hopes of little peoples through expected straits,
And press into the final seal a sign that peace will come for longer than posterities can see ahead,
That man unto his fellow man shall be a friend forever."
—Norman Corwin, "On a Note of Triumph," 1945

164

• THE HAMMER SONG •

by Lee Hays and Pete Seeger*

2. If I had a bell, I'd ring
      it in the morning,
   I'd ring it in the
      evening—all over
      this land.
   I'd ring out danger, I'd
      ring out warning,
   I'd ring out love
      between my brothers
      and my sisters
   All over this land.

3. If I had a song, I'd sing
      it in the morning,
   I'd sing it in the
      evening—all over
      this land.
   I'd sing out danger, I'd
      sing out warning,
   I'd sing out love
      between my brothers
      and my sisters
   All over this land.

4. Well, I've got a
      hammer, and I've got
      a bell,
   And I've got a song—
      all over this land,
   It's the hammer of
      justice, it's the bell of
      freedom,
   It's the song about love
      between my brothers
      and my sisters
   All over this land.

*This song never went anywhere till Peter, Paul and Mary changed my original melody. But I've discovered that you can sing my old melody or theirs, or half a dozen others, all at the same time, and they harmonize with each other. There's a moral there, somewhere, I think.—P.S.

166

Instead, the veterans found massive unemployment. The factories, which had been busy turning out planes and tanks, closed to retool and readjust to the new peace-time economy.

"They've closed up Willow Run . . . they gave the workers Army-Navy E's and told them to go home because the Government and Mr. Ford didn't want the plant anymore. Nobody wants Willow Run, the 95 million dollar factory that produced almost 9,000 Liberator bombers. Nobody wants the 51,950 pieces of machinery. . . . And nobody wants the more than 20,000 human beings who go with the plant."
—The C.I.O. *Economic Outlook,* 1945

UNEMPLOYMENT COMPENSATION BLUES

by Les Pine
Adapted by Jerry Silverman

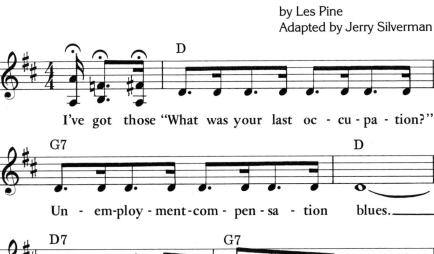

I've got those "What was your last oc - cu - pa - tion?"

Un - em-ploy - ment-com - pen - sa - tion blues._____

I've got those "How much mon-ey did you earn?

Stand in line and wait your turn" blues._____

_____ They make me feel I'm com - mit-ting a sin_____

_____ To get back part of what I paid

in. I've got those "Have you had an in - ter - view?_____

A7

D   G7   D

Come back in a week or two" blues._____

2. I've got those unemployment-compensation
   "Please fill out an application" blues.
   I've got those "State your weekly minimum.
   You don't wanna work, you bum" blues.
   And when I'm through with my weekly
   routine, I spend my money on Thorazine.
   I've got those by-the-time-I-get-my-check,
   I-become-a-nervous-wreck blues.

3. I've got those unemployment-compensation
   —It ain't worth the aggravation—blues.
   I've got those "Won't you wait? Just have a
   chair"; Nothin' in my Frigidaire blues.
   I'm tired of feelin' like a jerk. All I want is a
   chance to work
   And lose those out-of-work-humiliation,
   unemployment-compensation blues.

Strikes erupted across the country. The unions had never been stronger. Over 18 million men and women belonged to the A.F.L. and the C.I.O.—more union members than at any other time in our history. In the ten years between 1935 and 1945, union

170

membership had quadrupled. There were now over 3 million women in the unions, more than the total number of workers who had been organized in 1935. The unions were confident that they would be able to put things back on the right track. In 1946, four and a half million people marched in picket lines.

"FROM BULLETS TO BULL."
    —Picket sign, 1946, (quote)

• ROLL THE UNION ON •

by John Handcox and Lee Hays

*Multiple verses can be fabricated by replacement of "boss" with other subject—scab, sheriff, or whoever.

• NEWSPAPERMEN •

by Vern Partlow

Everyone was union-
izing—cowboys, un-
dertaker's helpers,
white-collar workers.

Newspapermen closed
their dailies. A reporter
on the *Los Angeles
News* exchanged his
typewriter for a guitar

Oh, news-pa-per-men meet such in-ter-est-ing

peo-ple!_____ They know the low-down;

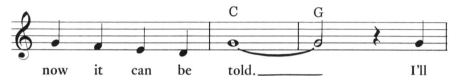

now it can be told._____ I'll

tell you, quite re-li-a-bly, off the re-cord___

_____ A-bout some charm-ing peo-ple I have

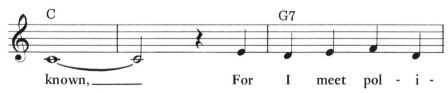

known,_____ For I meet pol-i-

ti-cians and graft-ers by the score,

Kill-ers plain and fan-cy; it's real-ly quite a

and led the Newspaper
Guild picket line around
and around his paper.

We would "rather be
craftsmen . . . than left
down in the valley of
ragged individualism."
—Ed Angley, a
founding member
of N.G.A.

bore. Oh, news-pa-per-men meet such in-ter-est-ing

peo - ple! _____ They wal - low in cor -

rup-tion, crime, and gore. Ting-a-ling-a-ling. Cit-y

desk, hold the press, hold the press. Ex - tra,

ex - tra, read all a-bout it! It's a mess, meets the

test. Yes, news-pa-per-men meet such in-ter-est-ing

peo - ple! _____ It's won - der - ful to

rep - re - sent the press.

2. Now you remember Mrs. Sadie Smuggery:
   She needed money to buy a new fur coat.
   To get insurance, she employed
        skullduggery;
   She up and cut her husband's only throat.
   She chopped him into fragments and stuck
        them in a trunk;
   She shipped it to her uncle back yonder in
        Podunk.
   Oh, newspapermen meet such interesting
        people!
   It must have startled poor old Sadie's unc.
        Ting-a-ling-a-ling . . . . .

3. Yes, newspapermen meet such interesting
        people!
   I've met the girl with million-dollar knees,
   Also the guy who sat five years upon a
        steeple;
   Just where the point was, I could never see.
   I've met Capone and Hoover and lots of
        other fakes;
   I've even met a genius who swallows
        rattlesnakes.
   Oh, newspapermen meet such interesting
        people—
   Like the richest girl who could not bake a
        cake.
        Ting-a-ling-a-ling . . . . .

4. Oh, publishers are such interesting people!
   Their policy's an acrobatic thing.
   They claim to represent the common people;
   It's funny Wall Street never has complained.
   But publishers have worries, for publishers
        must go
   To working folks for readers and big shots
        for their dough.
   Oh, publishers are such interesting people!
   It could be prostitution—I don't know.
        Ting-a-ling-a-ling, advertising!
        Ting-a-ling-a-ling, circulation!
        Get that payoff! Keep those readers!
        What a headache; what a mess!
   Yes, publishers are such interesting people!
   Let's give three cheers for freedom of the
        press.

5. Oh, newspapermen are such interesting
        people!
   They used to work like hell just for romance,

But finally, the movies notwithstanding,
They all got tired of patches on their pants,
They organized a union to get a living wage.
They joined progressive actors upon a living
     stage.
Now newspapermen meet such interesting
     people
Who know they've got a people's fight to
     wage.
     Ting-a-ling-a-ling, Newspaper Guild!
     We got a free new world to build.
     Meet the people—that's a thrill.
     All together fits the bill.
Oh, newspapermen meet such interesting
     people!
It's wonderful to represent the Guild.

176

But without the wartime pressure, strikes dragged on. When companies did settle, according to Thomas Brooks, they used the wage boosts "as a fulcrum for raising prices. . . . The unions served as perfect scapegoats." The familiar wage–price spiral of postwar America was on, and public opinion blamed the unions.

Walter Reuther of the U.A.W. insisted that General Motors open its books and prove that it could not raise wages without raising prices. G.M. refused and, with several other large corporations, began a campaign to limit union power.

"The problems of the United States can be summed up in two words: Russia abroad, labor at home."
—Charles Erwin Wilson,
president, General Motors
Corporation, 1946

Conservative Congressmen who had reluc-

tantly put up with labor's growing influence through the Roosevelt years promoted legislation to curtail unions' growth. In 1947 they succeeded by passing the Taft-Hartley Act.

Though meant to balance the power of labor and management, the act actually repealed many of the hard-won protections that labor had gained during the 1930s. Among other provisions, Taft-Hartley outlawed mass picketing, denied unions the right to contribute to political campaigns, prohibited boycotts, and gave employers a right to interfere with attempts of employees to join trade unions.

One clause which unions found especially noxious gave individual states the right to "override provisions of the national labor law." Companies with antiunion policies would find a haven in these "right-to-work" states.

The "Labor Era" which had begun in the mid 1930s ended. With only one out of every four American workers a member of a trade union, the drive to organize the unorganized ran into a stone wall.

• BANKS OF MARBLE •

by Les Rice

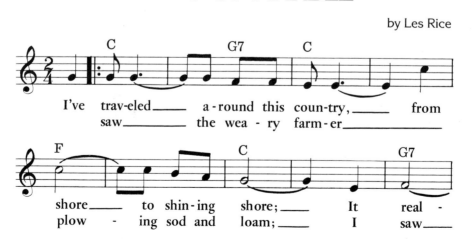

I've trav-eled _____ a-round this coun-try, _____ from
saw _____ the wea-ry farm-er _____

shore _____ to shin-ing shore; _____ It real -
plow - ing sod and loam; _____ I saw _____

3. I saw the seamen standing idly by the shore;
   I heard the bosses saying, "Got no work for
   you no more."

   But the banks are made of marble,
   With a guard at every door,
   And the vaults are stuffed with silver
   That the seamen sweated for.

4. I saw the weary miner scrubbing coal dust
   from his back.
   I heard his children crying, "Got no coal to
   heat the shack."

   But the banks are made of marble,
   With a guard at every door,

And the vaults are stuffed with silver
That the miner sweated for.

5. I've seen good people working throughout
   this mighty land,
   I prayed we'd get together, and together
   make a stand.

FINAL CHORUS:
Then we'd own those banks of marble,
with a guard at every door,*
And we'd share those vaults of silver
that we have sweated for!

* Don McLean says if you're fighting for a fair and just world,
  there would be "*no* guard at any door."

179

Under increasing pressure from right-wing groups at home and the Cold War abroad, the fragile coalition of radicals, progressives, and traditional unionists which had steered the unions through their years of growth began to break up. Some unions began to purge their ranks of the left-wing organizers and officials who had done much to build unionism in the 1930s.

The anti-Communist "witch-hunt hysteria" that swept across America in the late 1940s and early 1950s was echoed within the unions. Between 1949 and 1951 the C.I.O. threw out eleven unions with almost a million members, because the unions' leaders were supposedly Communist.

"This was called the Time of the Toad. Stool pigeons of the FBI and un-American committees came into the open to strut their stuff. Psychopathic 'reds' became psychopathic 'redbaiters': others went to pieces. Former radicals wilted under inquisition, confessing, recanting, giving lists of erstwhile comrades and friends. A peculiar moral degradation was setting in."

—Len De Caux, *Labor Radical*, 1970

" I dont care what kind of communist you are...
You reds are all the same to me..."

• THE INVESTIGATOR'S SONG •

by Harold Rome

Slowly, with rhythm

I've got a prob-lem__ that is both-er-ing me.

I've got a real un-sol-u-ble mys-ter-y. It would

stun G. K. Ches-ter-ton, foil Con-an Doyle, drive Sher-lock Holmes to the

wall, Stump Hum-phrey Bo-gart and Ba-call!

CHORUS

Who's gon-na in-ves-ti-gate the man who in-ves-ti-gates the

man who in-ves-ti-gates me? I don't doubt my

loy-al-ty,__ But how a-bout what his may be?__

Who'll check the rec-ord of the man who checks the rec-ord of the

man who checks the rec-ord of mine? Seems to me__ there's

Extra patters:

2. Maybe they won't like the books he's reading,
   Or the way he wants to pray.
   Maybe he won't have the proper breeding
   Maybe he ran T.V.A.
   Believe me brother, THAT'S OU-TRAY!

3. Maybe he's the kind does his own thinking;
   Maybe tries to use his head.
   Maybe he goes in for vodka drinking.
   Maybe his corpuscles are red.
   Believe me, brother, OFF WITH HIS HEAD!

"My husband has been out of work for 14 months. He worked hard at a union mine at Leatherwood. Now the company has terminated the union contract and plans to go back to work with scab workers. It just isn't here that all this is happening. The company will say they have to close as they are going in the hole. Then they will reopen with scab laborers that will work for nothing as long as the boss smiles at them and gives them a pat on the back. . . . All we want is a decent wage and good insurance that will help our families. Is that too much to ask?

—Letter from Clara Sullivan,
Scuddy, Kentucky

Riding the wave of antiunion feeling, using loopholes created by the Taft-Hartley Law, companies laid off union workers and brought in nonunion replacements.

"My dad never saw real money. He was constantly in debt to the coal company.

When shopping was needed, Dad would go to a window and draw little brass tokens against his account. They could only be spent at the company store. He used to say, "I can't afford to die; I owe my soul to the company store."

—Merle Travis

• SIXTEEN TON •

by Merle Travis

With a driving beat

Now, some peo-ple say a man's made out of mud,— But a poor man's made out of mus-cle and blood, mus-cle and blood, skin and bones,— a mind that's weak and a back that's strong.—

CHORUS

You load six-teen ton and what do you get?—You get an-oth-er day old-er and deep-er in debt,— Saint Pe-ter, don't you call me 'cause I can't go,— I

owe__ my soul to the com - pa - ny store.

2. I was born one morning when the sun didn't
    shine.
   I picked up my shovel and I walked to the
    mine.
   I loaded sixteen ton of number nine coal,
   And the straw boss hollered,
   "Well, bless my soul!"
                      CHORUS

3. I was born one morning in the drizzling rain.
   Fighting and trouble is my middle name.
   I was raised in the bottoms by a momma
    hound;
   I'm mean as a dog, but I'm gentle as a lamb.
                      CHORUS

4. If you see me coming, you better step aside.
   A lot of men didn't, and a lot of men died.
   I got a fist of iron and a fist of steel;
   If the right one don't get you,
   Then the left one will.
                      CHORUS

Unable to organize new workers effectively, afraid to pursue large social issues, the unions concentrated on "pork-chop issues" —cost-of-living wage increases and job security. But when industry hit the skids in 1949, millions of workers were out on the streets again looking for work.

"Being part of something, making something happen, was important. That's the difference between being alive and being dead. Now I'm not making anything happen."
—Unemployed woman (Barbara Terwilliger), quoted in *Working* by Studs Terkel

• WHEN A FELLOW IS OUT OF A JOB •

Words by John Barnes   Music by Grant Rogers

All na - ture is sick from her heels to her

hair When a fel - low is out of a job.

* The key of G is probably too high for a low-key song. Try it down in D.

She's all out of kil-ter,— be-yond all re-pair When a fel-low is out of a job.— —There's no juice in the earth,— no salt in the sea,— no gin-ger in life in this land of the free, And the un-i-verse ain't what it's cracked up to be When a fel-low is out of a job.——

2. What's the good of blue skies and
     blossoming trees
   When a fellow is out of a job?
   And your kids have big patches all over their
     knees
   When a fellow is out of a job.
        Those patches you see look as big as the
          sky;
        They blot out the landscape and cover
          your eye,
        And the sun can't shine through the best it
          may try
   When a fellow is out of a job.

3. Ev'ry man that's a man wants to help push
     the world,
   But he can't if he's out of a job.
   He's left out behind, on the shelf he is
     curled,
   When a fellow is out of a job.
        He feels he's no part in the whole of the
          plan,
        An obsolete cog, only half of a man,
        And the world isn't what he's had it to
          plan
   When a fellow is out of a job.

   Repeat first chorus:
   "There's no juice, etc."

186

The Mills

In some Southern states, companies persuaded state legislatures to ban union shops. Working conditions deteriorated quickly.

"I love to work. But they just about kill you there now. They're speeding up the machines all the time, stretchin' them out. They're like to kill you. . . . We ain't got but fifteen minutes to go to the bathroom and eat dinner. So you know what I do? I get a cup of water . . . right out of the spigot."
　　　　—Lilian Harrel, textile worker, quoted in *Rise Gonna Rise*
　　　　by Mimi Conway, Doubleday, 1979

• THE MILL WAS MADE OF MARBLE •

by Joe Glazer

I dreamed that I had died _____ and gone to my ____ re - ward: _____ A job in heav - en's tex - tile plant on a gold - en bou - le - vard. _____

CHORUS

The mill was made of mar - ble, _____ the ma- chines were made out of gold, _____ And

no - bod - y   ev - er   got   tired,_____   and

no - bod - y   ev - er   grew   old._____

2. This mill was built in a garden—no dust or lint could be found.
The air was so fresh and so fragrant, with flowers and trees all around.
   CHORUS

3. It was quiet and peaceful in heaven—there was no clatter or boom.
You could hear the most beautiful music as you worked at the spindle and loom.
   CHORUS

4. There was no unemployment in heaven; we worked steady all through the year;
We always had food for our children; we never were haunted by fear.
   CHORUS

5. When I woke from this dream about heaven, I wondered if someday there'd be
A mill like that one down below here on earth, for workers like you and like me.
   CHORUS

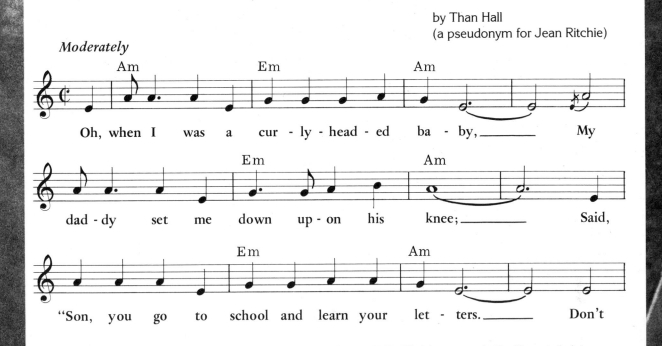

• THE L AND N DON'T STOP HERE ANYMORE •

by Than Hall
(a pseudonym for Jean Ritchie)

Moderately

Oh, when I was a cur-ly-head-ed ba-by,_____ My

dad-dy set me down up-on his knee;_____ Said,

"Son, you go to school and learn your let-ters._____ Don't

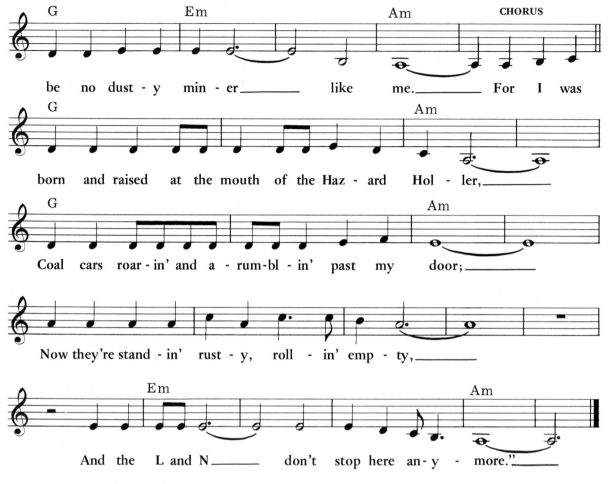

be no dust-y min-er_____ like me._____ For I was born and raised at the mouth of the Haz-ard Hol-ler,_____ Coal cars roar-in' and a-rum-bl-in' past my door;_____ Now they're stand-in' rust-y, roll-in' emp-ty,_____ And the L and N_____ don't stop here an-y-more."_____

2. I used to think my daddy was a black man
   With scrip enough to buy the company store,
   But now he goes downtown with empty
     pockets
   And his face as white as February snow.
   CHORUS

3. Last night I dreamt I went down to the office
   To get my pay just like I done before;
   Kudzu vines* had covered up the doorway,
   And there was trees and grass a-growin'
     through the floor.
   CHORUS

4. I never thought I'd live to love the coal dust;
   Never thought I'd pray to hear the tipple
     roar.
   But, Lord, how I wish that grass could
     change to money,
   Them greenbacks fill my pockets once more!
   CHORUS

* Kudzu vines had been imported from Japan as a ground
  cover for the spoilbanks from new highways and strip
  mines.

To survive, the larger unions merged into large corporate structures, negotiating industry-wide contracts. In 1955, the rival A.F.L. and C.I.O. became one huge union. But in the new union bureaucracies the grievances of individual members started to fall through the cracks. More and more the cry began to be heard "The union doesn't care!"

192

"The leaders of our union have let the old coal miners down. They're fixin' to let the young ones down. . . . The union don't belong up in Washington. We ain't got any coal mines up there."

—Nimrod Workman, miner,
quoted in *Voices from the Mountains*

During the 1950s, another disaster rocked labor: a Senate subcommittee under John McClellan discovered evidence of racketeering in three major unions. The accused labor leaders, guilty and innocent, were dragged onto national television. Though only a few unions were corrupt, the media portrayed a labor movement rife with crime. For years to come, the public image of the labor leader was not the crusader or organizer, but the cigar-chomping gangster on TV.

Union membership began to shrink. By the end of the 1950s, the business community was again reporting the demise of the unions.

"Organized labor . . . is growing weaker. The unions have simply stopped growing: The labor force continues to expand, but in areas (e.g., the South) and in occupations (e.g., white-collar work) that have traditionally resisted unionism. Only a few union leaders seem to be aware of this. . . . The sad fact is that the United States labor movement . . . can no longer claim that it is reforming our society or even that it speaks for the underprivileged."

—"What really ails the unions?",
Fortune magazine, October 1959

But a new phase of the movement was just beginning.

"Down at the mill, they didn't let us drink out of the cooler. We couldn't have no water unless we brought a glass or a bottle from home to run water in. A black woman who was sweeping over there, Semora Sweat, brought a glass from home for us to drink out of. Our supervisor, Gerald Cross, throwed it in the trash can. Miss Sweat came over to me. 'How we gonna drink water?' is what she said. I said, 'I'm gonna drink water just like they do'; so I started drinking out of the cooler."

—Otis Edwards interviewed in
Rise Gonna Rise

This next song is descended from a folk version of an Afro-American hymn, "I Will Overcome." It was turned into a union song, "We Will Overcome," by black tobacco workers. In the 1940s, Zilphia Horton, a white woman, learned it and taught it to others at a Tennessee labor school, now the Highlander Center. Guy Carawan then taught it to the founding convention of S.N.C.C.* in 1960. All royalties go to a non-profit fund supporting black music in the South.

I confess that for me the most important word in this song is "We," and when I sing it, I think of the whole human race which must stick together if we are going to solve the problems of war and peace, of poverty, ignorance, fear of health and population. When I feel low and pessimistic about the human species, I occasionally find myself humming it at work.

—P.S.

* Student Nonviolent Coordinating Committee.

"If we had said we were going to overcome next week, it would be a little unrealistic. What will we sing the week after next?"
—Bernice Reagan,
   musician, civil rights worker,
   director, Afro-American Studies,
   Smithsonian Institution

• WE SHALL OVERCOME •

New words and arrangement by Zilphia Horton,
Frank Hamilton, Guy Carawan and Pete Seeger

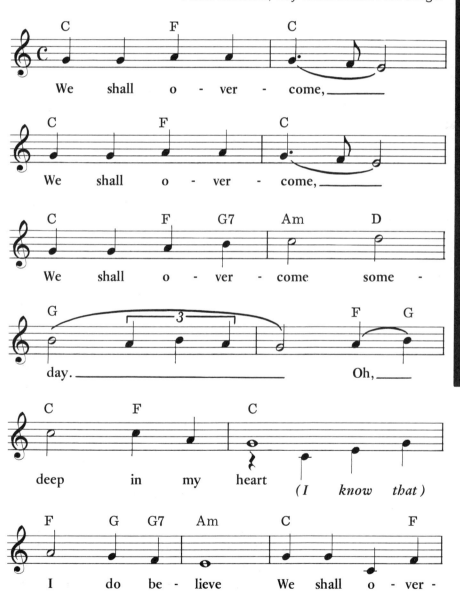

We shall o-ver-come,_____
We shall o-ver-come,_____
We shall o-ver-come some-day._____ Oh,_____
deep in my heart (I know that)
I do be-lieve We shall o-ver-

come   some - day. _____

2. We'll walk hand in hand,
   We'll walk hand in hand,
   We'll walk hand in hand someday.
   Oh, deep in my heart
   I do believe
   WE SHALL OVERCOME someday.

3. We shall live in peace . . .

4. We shall all be free . . .

5. We are not afraid . . . (Today!)

6. The whole wide world around . . .

7. Black and white together . . . (Now!)

8. WE SHALL OVERCOME . . .

(Of course, each songleader will make his or her selection of verses from the hundreds of verses that have been sung by now. Like "Roll the Union On" and "We Shall Not Be Moved," this song is never sung exactly the same twice.—P.S.)

CHAPTER 6
MORE THAN A PAYCHECK
1963–Now

"Union Power Plus Soul Power Equals Victory!"
—Slogan of South Carolina hospital workers

In 1776, our new nation had only three million inhabitants. Two centuries later, over a hundred million hardworking men and women are building roads, repairing bridges, growing crops, sending information, moving freight and passengers.

Jobs have changed, but many problems have only taken new guises: dangerous jobs have moved to the cotton mills and chemical factories; prideless jobs fill offices and assembly lines; jobs can still be snatched away in a second, when a multinational corporation closes a plant and moves its capital into more profitable avenues.

"Either it makes money, or out it goes!"
—Samuel B. Casey, Jr., president,
Pullman-Standard Corporation,

Unions are going through one of their periodic crises. Because of restrictive legislation and difficulties organizing new industries, unions now represent fewer than 25 percent of working Americans.

But the people haven't changed. The same spirit that built the country can be heard everywhere. Many working people want to participate more, not only in union decisions but in management decisions at the place where they work. Voices that have remained nearly silent for years are speaking with a new and powerful sound.

"With a delicate motion of the hand and wrist you urge the arc along the joint, adding molten filler metal, drop by drop. The welding power comes from a generator to the torch like a tiny lightning bolt that you hold in your hand. . . . The arc melts a region of the joint. All your attention is directed at this puddle of steel, about the size of a child's fingernail, inches away from your face. For the welder, intent on the moment, with the hiss of the argon gas purge blowing through the torch head, with the slight high-pitched buzz of the arc and its ionizing ozonous odor, its penetrating brilliance . . . casting shadows on the walls of the booth, the process is hypnotizing, fascinating."
   —Potter Wickware, welder, *The New York Times,* 1979

"The foreman said, 'I would not let my wife come out here and do this kind of work!' And I said, 'I'm not asking you to let your wife come out here and do it. But I'd like for you to let me come and do it!'. . . . The men there really thought it was a big joke. . . . The foreman sent us over to take the Bethlehem welding test. And I think everyone in the shipyard had been alerted because I never saw so many people around. . . . My friend and I knew we could weld. There wasn't any question about it! We took the test, and sure enough we really knew what to do with the welding rod!"
   —Thelma Carthen, welder, quoted in *Conversations* by Terry Wetherby, Les Femmes Press, 1977

198

• I'M GONNA BE AN ENGINEER •

Constructed by Peggy Seeger

Easily - not too fast

When I was a lit - tle girl, I wished I was a boy. I

tagged a - long be - hind the gang and wore me cor - du - roys.

Ev - 'ry - bod - y said I on - ly did it to an - noy, but I was

gon - na be an en - gi - neer.

Ma - ma told me, "Can't you be a la - dy? Your

du - ty is to make me the moth - er of a pearl.

Wait un - til you're old - er, dear, and may - be

Fine

you'll be glad that you're a girl."

(This part only after verses 1, 3, 6 and 7.)

Dain - ty as a Dres-den stat - ue,—

gen - tle as a Jer - sey cow—

Smooth as silk,— gives cream - y milk.—

Learn to coo.— Learn to moo.—

That's what to do to be a la - dy now.—

2. When I went to school, I learned to write
   and how to read,
   History, geography—and home economy.
   *(Next two lines repeat melody of first two
   lines)*
   And typing is a skill that every girl is sure to
   need
   To while away the extra time until the time
   to breed.
   And then they had the nerve to say,
   "What would you like to be?"
   I says, "I'm gonna be an engineer!"

   No, you only need to learn to be a lady.
   The duty isn't yours for to try and run the
   world.
   An engineer could never have a baby!
   Remember, dear, that you're a girl.

3. So I become a typist and I study on the sly.
   Working out the day and night so I can
   qualify,
   And every time the boss come in, he pinched
   me on the thigh,
   Says, "I've never had an engineer!"

   You owe it to the job to be a lady.
   It's the duty of the staff for to give the
   boss a whirl.
   The wages that you get are crummy,
   maybe,
   But it's all you get, 'cause you're a girl.

   She's smart! (for a woman). I wonder how
   she got that way?
   You get no choice, you get no voice,
   Just stay mum, pretend you're dumb,
   That's how you come to be a lady today!

4. Then Jimmy came along and we set up a
      conjugation;
   We were busy every night with loving
      recreation.
   I spent my day at work so he could get his
      education,
   And now he's an engineer!

        He says "I know you'll always be a lady.
        It's the duty of my darling to love me all
           my life.
        Could an engineer look after or obey me?
        Remember, dear, that you're my wife!"

5. As soon as Jimmy got a job, I studied hard
      again.
   Then, busy at my turret-lathe a year or so,
      and then,
   The morning that the twins were born,
      Jimmy says to them,
   "Kids, your mother was an engineer."

        You owe it to the kids to be a lady,
        Dainty as a dishrag, faithful as a chow.
        Stay at home; you got to mind the baby.
        Remember, you're a mother now.

6. Every time I turn around there's something
      else to do—
   Cook a meal or mend a sock or sweep a floor
      or two.
   Listen in to Jimmy Young—it makes me
      want to spew!
   I was gonna be an engineer!

        I really wish that I could be a lady;
        I could do the lovely things that a lady's
           s'posed to do.
        I wouldn't even mind, if only they would
           pay me
        And I could be a person too!

What price—for a woman? You can buy her
   for a ring of gold;
To love and obey (without any pay);
You get a cook and a nurse (for better or
   worse).
You don't need a purse when a lady is sold.

7. But now that times are harder and my
      Jimmy's got the sack,
   I went down to Vickers. They were glad to
      have me back;
   I'm a third-class citizen, my wages tell me
      that,
   But I'm a first-class engineer!

        The boss, he says, "I pay you as a lady;
        You only got the job 'cause I can't afford a
           man.
        With you I keep the profits as high as may
           be;
        You're just a cheaper pair of hands!"

You got one fault! You're a woman. You're
   not worth the equal pay.
A bitch or a tart, you're nothing but heart;
Shallow and vain, you got no brain;
Go down the drain like a lady today!

8. I listened to my mother and I joined a typing
      pool;
   I listened to my lover and I put him through
      his school;
   If I listen to the boss, I'm just a bloody
      fool—
   And an underpaid engineer!

        I been a sucker ever since I was a baby,
        As a daughter, as a lover, as a mother and
           a "dear,"
        But I'll fight them as a woman, not a lady,
        I'll fight them as an engineer.

• COAL TATTOO •

by Billy Edd Wheeler

Briskly

Trav - el - in' down that coal - town— road;

Lis - ten to my rub - ber tires whine.

Good-bye to buck-eye and white syc - a - more—

I'm leav - in' you be - hind.

I've been a coal man all my life,

Lay - in' down— track in the hole._____ Got a

back like an iron - wood bent by the wind,

Blood veins blue as the coal.

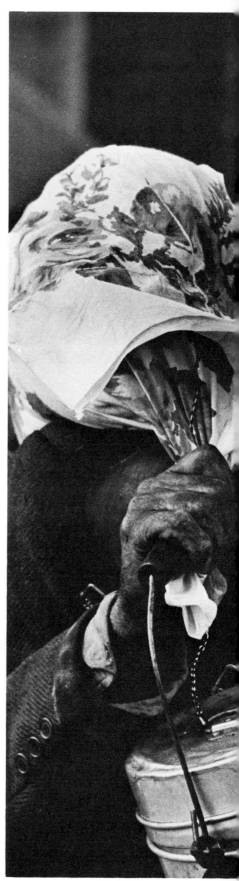

2. Somebody said,
   That's a strange tattoo
   You have on the side of your head.
   I said, That's the blueprint left by the coal;
   Just a little more and I'd been dead.
   But I love the rumble and I love the dark.
   I love the cool of the slate.
   But it's travelin' down that new road lookin'
      for a job,
   This travelin' and lookin', I hate.

3. I've stood for the union, walked in the line,
   Fought against the company
   I've stood for the U.M.W. of A.
   Now who's gonna stand for me?
   For I got no house and I got no pay;
   Just got a worried soul
   And this blue tattoo on the side of my head
   Left by the number nine coal.

4. Someday when I'm dead and gone
   To heaven, the land of my dreams,
   I won't have to worry about losin' my job
   To bad times and big machines.
   I won't have to pay my money away
   And lose my hospital plans;
   I'm gonna cut coal while the blue heavens
      roll
   And sing with the angel band.

With the finding of cheap oil, the deep mines closed. When the cheap oil went, the mines reopened. Then the veins ran out. The deep mines gave way to strip mines. Life in the coal belt changed and changed and changed again. Miners were not only jobless now, they were homeless.

"We all left Letcher County for the same reason: to find work. . . . If enough work was available in Letcher County, 99 percent of us would come home."
—Jim Cornett, quoted in *Voices from the Mountains* by Guy and Candide Carawan, Knopf 1975

203

In 1940, the average American lived for sixty years. The mandatory retirement age was 60. By 1984 an American could expect to live to 72. The average forced retirement was 63.

"I was a shipping clerk for twenty-five years. The firm went kerflooey. Then I put in fifteen years at a felt works. I was operating a cutting machine. . . . I get $36 a month [pension] and I get $217 from Social Security. . . . I'm hopin' to be around here for at least another five years. I don't care. Twenty more years? Oh, God, *no!*"

—Joe Zmuda,
quoted in *Working*
by Studs Terkel

• ALL USED UP •

by Utah Phillips

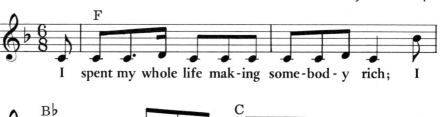

I spent my whole life mak-ing some-bod - y rich; I

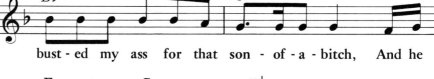

bust - ed my ass for that son - of - a - bitch, And he

left me to die like a dog in a ditch And

told me I'm all used up._____ He
used up my la-bor, he used up my time, He
plun-dered my bod-y and squan-dered my mind And
gave me a pen-sion of hand-outs and wine And
told me I'm all used up._____

2. My kids are in hock to a God you call work,
   Slaving their lives out for some other jerk;
   My youngest in Frisco just made shipping
   clerk
   And he don't know I'm all used up.
   Young people reaching for power and gold
   Don't have respect for anything old.
   For pennies they're bought and for promises
   sold.
   Someday they'll all be used up.

3. They use up the oil, they use up the trees,
   They use up the air, and they use up the sea;
   Well, how about you, friend, and how about
   me?
   What's left when we're all used up?
   I'll finish my life in this crummy hotel.
   It's lousy with bugs, and my God, what a
   smell!
   But my plumbing still works and I'm clear as
   a bell.
   Don't tell me I'm all used up.

4. Outside my window the world passes by;
   It gives me a handout and spits in my eye,
   And no one can tell me, 'cause no one knows
   why,
   I'm livin', but I'm all used up.
   Sometimes in my dreams I sit by a tree;
   My life is a book of how things used to be,
   And kids gather 'round and they listen to me,
   And they don't think I'm all used up.

5. And there's songs and there's laughter and
   things I can do,
   And all that I've learned I can give back to
   you;
   I'd give my last breath just to make it come
   true—
   No, I'm not all used up.
   They use up the oil and they use up the
   trees,
   They use up the air and they use up the sea;
   Well, how about you, friend, and how about
   me?
   What's left when we're all used up?

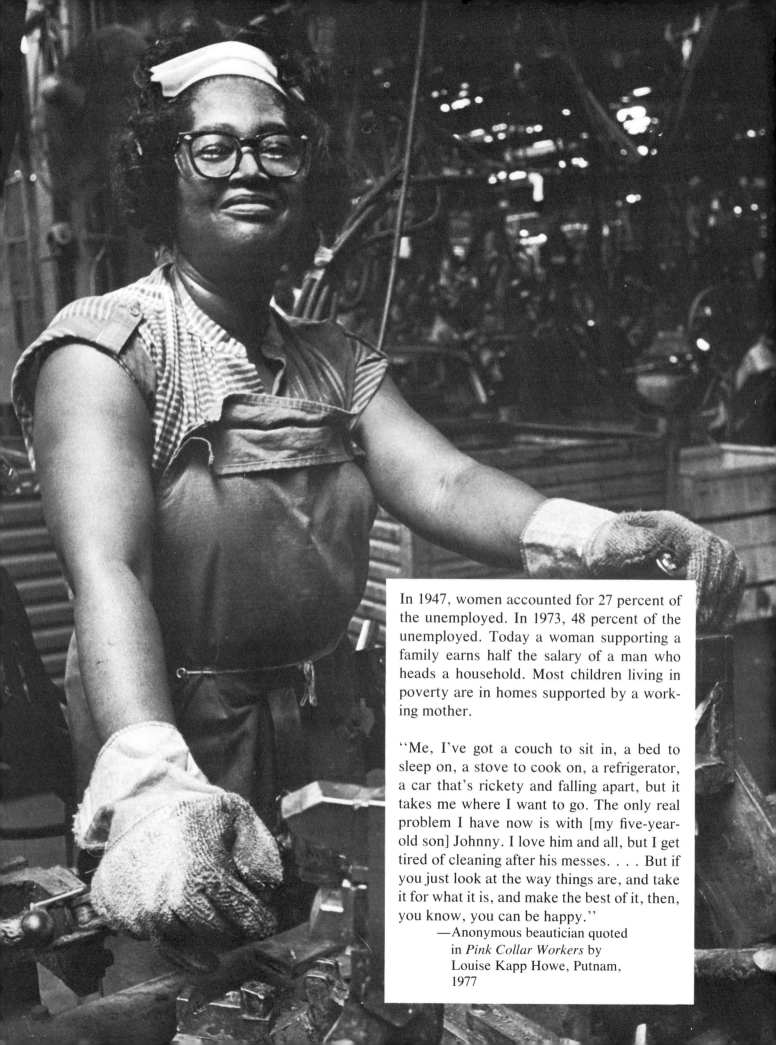

In 1947, women accounted for 27 percent of the unemployed. In 1973, 48 percent of the unemployed. Today a woman supporting a family earns half the salary of a man who heads a household. Most children living in poverty are in homes supported by a working mother.

"Me, I've got a couch to sit in, a bed to sleep on, a stove to cook on, a refrigerator, a car that's rickety and falling apart, but it takes me where I want to go. The only real problem I have now is with [my five-year-old son] Johnny. I love him and all, but I get tired of cleaning after his messes. . . . But if you just look at the way things are, and take it for what it is, and make the best of it, then, you know, you can be happy."
— Anonymous beautician quoted
in *Pink Collar Workers* by
Louise Kapp Howe, Putnam,
1977

These lyrics were originally sung to the tune of a popular country song called "Silver Threads and Golden Needles," but we couldn't get permission to print it, so I've adapted a traditional Irish melody to fit the words.

—P.S.

• BALLAD OF A WORKING MOTHER •

Words by Marilyn Major

say I should be hap-py that my pay it ain't too bad. They for-

get I'm the on - ly par - ent that my kids have ev - er had.

2. I hired a baby-sitter; she made near as much
      as me.
   She watched the television while my babies,
      they ran free.
   Well, I finally found a good one,
      and she treated them just fine;
   But it hurt to see them give her all the love
      that should be mine.
   <small>CHORUS</small>

3. As the years went by, I learned my job and
      half the men's jobs too.
   They liked to let me use their tools just to
      see what I could do.

They'd pat me on the fanny and they'd tell
   me I was cute;
For a decent job with equal pay that was
   sure some substitute!
   <small>CHORUS</small>

4. I went to see the foreman and I told him of
      my skills.
   I knew if I could get that job, it would help to
      pay my bills.
   Well, the foreman, he said, "Honey, we just
      can't do that. You see,
   That job is for a working man who has a
      family"!
   <small>CHORUS</small>

Migrant Farm Workers

Drawn from the poorest level of society—non–English-speaking immigrants or dispossessed tenant farmers—farm workers have been treated like livestock, herded into overcrowded dormitories or housed in shacks. In the prosperous 1960s, the average farm worker made less than $2,000 a year. The average life span was 49 years.

• DEPORTEE •

Woody Guthrie wrote "Deportees" after reading a report of a plane crash in Los Gatos, Mexico. The plane was flying home a group of Mexican workers who had entered the United States illegally, prompted by promises of high-paying jobs from unscrupulous growers in the California orchards. The newspaper didn't bother listing the names of those killed. Like surplus crops, they were just to get rid of.

Words by Woody Guthrie

Music by Marty Hoffman

The crops are all in, and the peach-es are rot - ting,____ The
or-ang - es are piled in their cre - o - sote dumps. You're
fly - ing them back to the Mex - i-can bor - der____ to
pay all their mon-ey to wade back a - gain.____ Good-bye to my
Juan,__ good - bye Ro-sa - li - ta; A - dios, mis a - mi-gos Je -

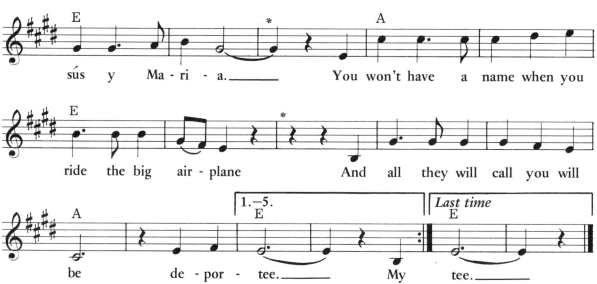

sús y Ma - ri - a._____ You won't have a name when you ride the big air - plane And all they will call you will be de - por - tee._____ My tee._____

* Measures can be added or subtracted at these points.

210

2. My father's own father, he waded that river.
   They took all the money he made in his life.
   My brothers and sisters come working the fruit trees,
   And they rode the truck till they took down and died.
   CHORUS

3. Some of us are illegal and some are not wanted.
   Our work contract's out, and we have to move on
   Six hundred miles to the Mexican border.
   They chase us like outlaws, like rustlers, like thieves.
   CHORUS

4. We died in your hills, we died in your deserts,
   We died in your valleys and died on your plains,
   We died 'neath your trees and we died in your bushes,
   Both sides of the river—we died just the same.
   CHORUS

5. The sky plane caught fire over Los Gatos canyon—
   A fireball of lightning which shook all our hills,
   Who are all these friends all scattered like dry leaves?
   The radio says they are just . . . deportees.
   CHORUS

6. Is this the best way we can grow our big orchards?
   Is this the best way we can grow our good fruit—
   To fall like dry leaves, to rot on my topsoil
   And be called by no name except deportees?
   CHORUS

In 1962, 300 crop pickers met in a hall in Fresno, California, and listened to a young Mexican-American propose a union of farm workers. Three years later, César Chávez helped lead 50,000 pickers in their first successful strike in California history.

"Red faced with anger, growers in neatly pressed khaki trousers paced restlessly at the borders of their vineyards, kicking at the dirt as the pickets circled them. . . . Behind them, the [nonstriking] workers moved through the rows of eye-level vines, feigning indifference or smiling weakly as the pickets demanded that they, too, join la Huelga . . . .

"Caravans of strikers and volunteers roved the back roads continuously, driving along the black ribbons of pancake-flat asphalt . . . hoping to discover where the growers had assigned work crews within the 38,000 acres of struck vineyards. . . . 'It's like striking a plant that has a thousand entrance gates and is forty square miles large,' noted Terry Cannon."
—From *A Long Time Coming* by
   Dick Meister and Anne Loftis,
   Macmillan

211

Through the years, the United Farm Workers patiently organized the rich farmlands of California, moving northward through the vineyards, southward through the vegetable and fruit lands, attracting national attention with their grass-roots democracy and their dedication to nonviolence.

Excluded by law from the protection of the National Labor Relations Board, the Farm Workers depended on publicity and on boycotts to make their point. Finally, in 1970, the growers agreed to recognize the union.

"The strike has been long. . . . The strikers have lost their homes and their cars. But I think that in losing their worldly possessions in order to serve the poor, they found themselves."

—César Chávez, Delano,
California, 1970

By the end of the 1970s, despite the attempts of some growers to divide the farm workers with interunion jurisdictional disputes, the United Farm Workers won collective-bargaining rights in California, higher wages, and better living conditions. But outside of California, pickers have as little as ever. Today, fewer than 10 percent of the farm workers in America have any union protection.

"My father
Could never write a poem,
But when he lined up his plow
With a pine tree on a distant hill,
He made a furrow
Straight as an arrow
Across the length of his labor.

"My father
Could not write very many words,
But when he brought in his crop
In the heat of a summer afternoon,
He created a poem from the earth."

—Anonymous Mexican poem

The theme song of the most militant strike of the last quarter-century speaks only of the colors and sounds of the earth, which are everyone's birthright.

212

• DE COLORES •
(In Colors)

Slowly, flowing *

Traditional Spanish song

* A second voice can sing two notes below the melody throughout this song.

2. Canta el gallo, canta el gallo con el quiri-
    quiri-quiri-quiri-quiri;
  La gallina, la gallina con el cara-cara-cara-
    cara-cara;
  Los polluelos, los polluelos con el pío-pío-
    pío-pío-pío;
  Y por eso los grandes amores de muchos
    colores me gustan a mí;
  Y por eso los grandes amores de muchos
    colores me gustan a mí.

(In colors, in colors the fields in the spring dress up. In colors, in colors the little birds come from far off. In colors, in colors the rainbow we see glistening; and that's why those big many-colored loves are what I like.

(The rooster, the rooster sings with his cock-a-doodle-a-doodle-a-doo; the hen, the hen with cackle-a-cackle-a-cackle-a-cack; the chicks, the chicks with their cheepy-cheepy-cheepy-cheep; and that's why those big many-colored loves are what I like.)

• THE TAXI SONG •

by Steve and Peter Jones

"I'm so tired. My bottom gets so . . . Oh, every muscle aches in my body. My legs and feet and ankles and so forth . . . My pedaling the gas and brake, gas and brake all the time . . ."

—Booker Page, taxi driver, from *Working* by Studs Terkel

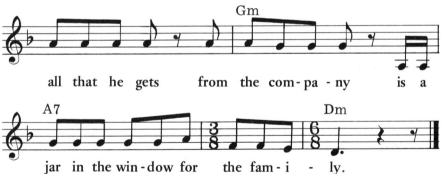

all that he gets from the com-pa-ny is a
jar in the win-dow for the fam-i-ly.

2. I read about it the very next day:
   He was sitting at Georgia and East-West Highway;
   He was hit by a drunk, and his body was tossed.
   He was dead on arrival at Holy Cross.
   CHORUS

3. That afternoon, like 'most ev'ry day,
   I drove up to the window to give them my pay:

"Here's what I owe you for driving your car,
And here is five dollars to go in the jar."
CHORUS

4. We drive the cabs until we're half dead,
   But the owner's the only one getting ahead.
   High off the hog is the way that he lives,
   And a jar in the window is all that he gives.
   CHORUS

Today's secretary was born in 1873, when the Remington company trained girls to demonstrate its new typing machine. It called the ladies "typewriters." The confusion between operator and machine has existed ever since.

Despite low pay, tenuous job security, frustrated expectations, and frequent mistreatment on the job, secretaries refused to unionize. In 1972 it could be said, "Secretaries' organizations. . . . are toothless and supportive of the status quo. The National Secretaries' Association is strongly reminiscent of the Girl Scouts—the same emphasis on duty, fidelity, loyalty."
—Mary Kathleen Benet, *The Secretarial Ghetto,* McGraw-Hill, 1972

But with the growth of depersonalized typing pools, complex new business machines, and management demand for higher and higher productivity, frustration boiled over. In 1980, a Boston working women's group called 9 to 5 began a campaign of picketing and publicity to establish minimum working conditions in the office.

"They should advance women further than they do, all the women. . . . As for computers, sure they should use them, but I'd see that people come first. And I'd see that workers weren't so competitive with each other. Women are trained to compete with each other to get the few really good jobs. . . . I believe there should be more human attitudes."
—Retired secretary, quoted in *Pink Collar Workers* by Louisa Kapp Howe, Putnam, 1977

• WORKIN' GIRL BLUES •

by Hazel Dickens

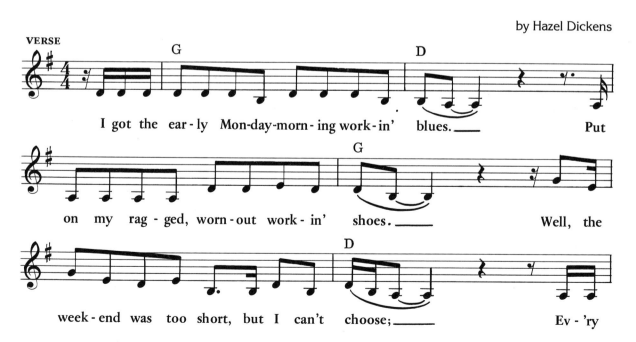

I got the ear-ly Mon-day-morn-ing work-in' blues.___ Put on my rag-ged, worn-out work-in' shoes.___ Well, the week-end was too short, but I can't choose;___ Ev-'ry

Mon-day brings these work-in' girl blues.___ I'm tired of work-in' my life a-way___ and giv-in' some-bod-y else all of my pay___ while they get rich on the prof-its that I lose,___ leav-in' me here_ with__ these work-in' girl blues.___

2. Well, the boss says a raise is due 'most any day,
But I wonder, Will my hair be all turned gray
Before he turns that money loose and I get my dues

And I lose a little bit of these workin' girl blues?
And I can't even afford a new pair of shoes,
While they can live in any old penthouse they choose,
And all that I got is the workin' girl blues.

• 9 to 5 •

From the 20th Century-Fox film "9 to 5"

by Dolly Parton

Tum - ble out of bed and stum - ble to the kitch - en,

Pour my - self a cup___ of am - bi - tion, And

yawn and stretch___ and try___ to come___ to life.___

Jump in the show - er and the blood starts pump - in';

Out in the street___ and the traf - fic starts jump - in' With

folks like me___ on the job from nine___ to five.___ Work - in'

nine to five___ what a way to make___ a liv - in', bare - ly

get - tin' by.___ It's all tak - in' and___ no giv - in'. They just use your mind___ and they

nev - er give___ you cred - it. It's e - nough to drive you cra - zy if___ you let it.

218

Only
Robinson Crusoe
Could Have Everything
Done By
Friday

CHORUS II:

Nine to five for service and devotion!
You would think that I would deserve a fair
    promotion;
Want to move ahead, but the boss won't
    seem to let me.
Sometimes I swear that man is out to get me.

They let you dream just to watch 'em shatter.
You're just a step on the boss's ladder,
But you've got dreams he'll never take away.
You're in the same boat with a lot of your
    friends,
Waiting for the day your ship'll come in.
The tide's gonna turn, and it'll all roll your way.

CHORUS

CHORUS III:

Nine to five—yeah, they got you where they
    want you.
There's a better world, and you think about
    it, don't you?
It's a rich man's game, no matter what they
    call it,
And you spend your life putting money in his
    wallet.

CHORUS

"I'm just a lawyer, you know. The companies employ me. Every time I do a good job, the union hollers that I'm a union buster. Hell—I am only doing my best!"
—Labor-relations lawyer, CBS Sunday Morning News, June 17, 1984

• THE UNION BUSTER •

Words by Paul McKenna

Tune: "Oh! Susanna"
by Stephen Foster

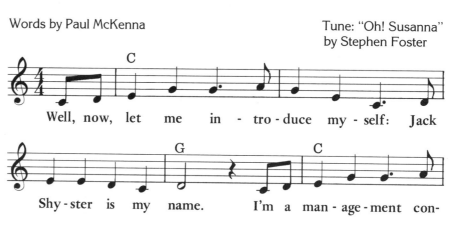

Well, now, let me in-tro-duce my-self: Jack
Shy-ster is my name. I'm a man-age-ment con-

sul - tant; un - ion bust - ing is my game. I'm a

mas - ter of the con job, I'm an ex - pert at the

hoax, and I make my liv - ing steal - ing bread from the

CHORUS

mouths of work - ing folks. I'm a un - ion bus - ter— the

boss - es' trust - y aide. I__ help keep their em-

ploy - ees o - ver-worked and un - der - paid.

2. In the old days we used gun thugs, we used ginks and finks and goons.
  Nowadays we use fancy words, but sing the same old tune—
  Pitting folks against each other, spreading hatred, fear, and lies,
  Cutting down the hopes of workers who rise up to organize.

3. There's no tactic I won't stoop to, there's no trick I haven't tried
  To manipulate the workers and to keep them petrified.

Texas Instruments, McDonald's, Litton Industries, Coors beer [*relevant substitutes are allowed*].
  I'm the man that they depend on to maintain their reign of fear.

4. Jack London tells the story: God was working in his lab,
  And with some hateful substance he made my good friend, the scab.
  Well, he gave some of that awful stuff a graduate degree;
  He dressed it in a three-piece suit, and that's how he made me.

221

"If an employee is scheduled for work and upon arrival at the job finds that there is no work, said employee may be sent home without compensation. . . .

"The company shall reserve the right to give lie-detector tests and take urinalysis of any worker at any time. . . . Refusal to submit to such tests may result in dismissal.

"The company reserves the right to strike 20 percent of the workers from the seniority records without cause."
— Concessions demanded of United Steelworkers by Pullman Company as alternative to closing the mill, 1982

"If they think we are going to lay down and die and give up everything labor has fought for, they've got to be crazy."
— Pullman worker, 1982

• HOW'D YOU LIKE TO GIVE A LITTLE BACK? •

by Larry Penn

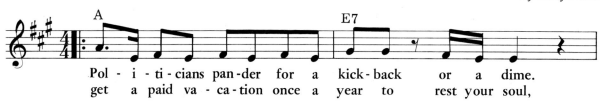

Pol - i - ti - cians pan - der for a kick - back or a dime.
get a paid va - ca - tion once a year to rest your soul,

Bus - 'ness un - der - stands it takes a lit - tle grease some-times.
A cost - of - liv - ing in - crease to keep you from the hole,

They must think that all of us are on the take like that.
And if they work you more than eight, you get time and one - half.

How'd you like to give a lit - tle back? You back?

CHORUS

How'd you like to give a lit - tle back? How'd you like to give a lit - tle

back, an' be a slave? How'd you like to give a lit - tle

back, an' be in chains? Af - ter all the time it took to

get what we have gained, How'd you like to give a lit - tle back?

3. It took a lot of struggle just to get some
     working rules
   And get a little muscle so they can't treat us
     like tools.
   Now the times are tougher, and they want to
     trim the fat.
   How'd you like to give a little back?

4. You have reached into the pockets of the
     corp'rate millionaire
   And finally got some wages that are close to
     being fair.
   It might have cut the profit, but at least he
     owed you that.
   How'd you like to give a little back?
                                    CHORUS

223

5. Union leaders tell us, ain't nothin' they can
    do—
   They're gonna take the plant and move away
    to Timbuktu.
   You'll be working for the Colonel, and
    McDonald's after that.
   How'd you like to give a little back?

6. I bought myself a guitar at the local music
    store,
   And it was made in places where they never
    were before.
   The merchant got the money, and the
    craftsman got the ax.
   How'd you like to give a little back?
                                    CHORUS

In the 1950's the Alexander Carpet Company left Yonkers, New York, and moved south to find cheap labor. Overnight nearly 7,000 people lost their jobs. In the 1970s, Otis Elevator closed its doors in the same city. Another 4,000 people out of work. The city went bankrupt. Throughout the North, factory after factory closed and moved, driven by concern for "the bottom line." One of the costs not calculated: human pain.

"The first week, I was out looking for something every day. Then it got to where the money situation only allowed me to go looking for work maybe once a week. I couldn't put gas in my car. . . . It wasn't long before everything was gone. Welfare started giving us $224 a month. . . . Sometimes we'd be completely flat zero broke. We ran out of food a couple of times. No money to buy food stamps. Wasn't nothing we could do. . . . We just didn't eat . . . sometimes for three, four days at a time."
          —Jim Hughes, quoted in *Not
            Working* by Harry Maurer, Holt
            Rinehart, 1979

224

• ARAGON MILL •

by Si Kahn

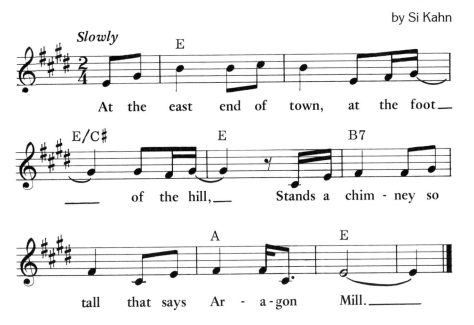

Slowly

At the east end of town, at the foot of the hill, Stands a chim-ney so tall that says Ar-a-gon Mill.

2. But there's no smoke at all coming out of the stack,
   For the mill has pulled out, and it ain't coming back.

3. Now I'm too old to work and I'm too young to die,
   And there's no place to go for my old man and I.

4. There's no children at all in the narrow, empty streets.
   Now the looms have all gone, it's so quiet, I can't sleep.

5. And the only tune I hear is the sound of the wind,
   As it blows through the town—weave and spin, weave and spin.

6. Now the mill has shut down. It's the only life I know.
   Tell me, where will I go? Tell me, where will I go?

7. And the only tune I hear is the sound of the wind,
   As it blows through the town—weave and spin, weave and spin.

"She does better than a hundred words a minute, she never forgets an appointment, she keeps records of all your expenses, she reminds you of your wife's birthday and remembers everything you tell her, she makes phone calls for you, she never gets sick, never makes a mistake, *and* she never gets pregnant!''
—Computer saleswoman at New
York computer show, 1983

"Now, they think the work is all being done by the machine. They come by and ask, 'Does your machine have time to do this'—like I'm just part of the machine. I always want to tell them, 'Don't ask me, ask the machine.' ''
—Computer operator, radio station
WBAI, New York, July 5, 1984

• FORGET-ME-NOT •
(a layoff lament)

by Arlene Mantle and collective session,
Humber Labor College, Ontario

Strident

We're still talk-ing a-bout build-ing strong un-ions,
Un-ions that will stretch from sea to sea. With high
tech and 6 and 5,* how the hell can we sur-vive? Look at
me— I'm lin-ing up for U. I. C.†

CHORUS

And I'm sing-ing, Sol-i-dar-i-ty For-ev-er,___ try-ing
hard to keep my un-ion spir-it high, But my
spir-it's al-most spent, and I can't pay the rent. Have you

*Wage controls.

†Unemployment insurance compensation.

ev - er seen a un - ion mem - ber cry?

2. For twenty years I worked in this factory;
   I thought that I had job security.
   But the robots have arrived,
   And the V.D.T.s have thrived,
   And there wasn't any room left there for me.
   CHORUS

3. If ever I needed my union,
   Lord knows I need it now.
   But I lost my vote, you see,
   And they lost track of me,

And the union's strength is weaker 'cause
I'm gone.
   CHORUS

4. Oh, you can force me out of the union,
   But you can't force the union out of me.
   For twenty years I've paid my dues,
   And I refuse
   To believe my union isn't there for me.
   CHORUS

229

"CS₂ (carbon disulfide): Both liquid and vapor are highly irritating to the skin, eyes, nose and air passages. This local irritation, however, is overshadowed by the serious long-term effects . . . High concentrations rapidly affect the brain, causing loss of consciousness and even death."

> —"OSHA: Dynamite for
> Workers," in Chip Hughes and
> Len Stanley, *Working Lives*,
> Pantheon, 1980

"Massey got this stuff worse than anybody. He is still barely living over near Canton. They give him a few more months before the cancer will eat up his brain. . . .

"George Sanders worked with us on the second floor, too. He used to empty those trash cans full of CS₂. Boy did he get a lot of fumes! I worked around him a week before he died."

> —Bert McColl quoted in "OSHA:
> Dynamite for Workers," *Ibid.*

"When you grow silicon crystals, you use arsenic, cyanide, and other chemicals to bake into silicon layers. . . . The workers are protected as little as possible."

> —Technician quoted in "Life on
> the Line—Silicon Valley's
> Anonymous Workers," by
> Kathy Chin, *Infoworld*, May 14,
> 1984

• HIGH TECH •

by Serious Bizness (Ngoma and Jaribu Hill)

Trips to the moon,— sat-el-lites,— sky-scrap-ers, and com-put-ers. This is— not— just a pass-in'— phase— it's part of the high— tech-nol-o-gy age.—

CHORUS

Check it— out,— find— out,— know what this tech-nol-o-gy is all a-bout.— You got a right to— know; find— out.—

Know what this tech-nol-o-gy is all a-bout.—

2. Little machines that look like T.V. sets store
      your memory.
   Don't forget the side effects—
   Little machines, gadgets, and such
   Can cause you job stress with every touch.
                    CHORUS

3. The boss is elated, the company's ecstatic.
   They think this high tech will make your
      work instamatic,
   Presto chango, right before your eyes!
   There are things you may not see, so don't
      be surprised.
                    CHORUS

4. Gotta make sure it's safe, make sure it's
      done right;
   Don't let speed and efficiency add misery to
      your life.
   Make sure it's safe, make sure it's done
      right;
   Don't let speed and efficiency add misery to
      your life.
   Chorus three times and fade out

231

STATE OF ILLINOIS—WORKMAN'S COMPENSATION SCHEDULE
(1976):

Ring finger..........	25 weekly installments totaling	$2,222.50
Little finger	120 weekly installments totaling	1,778.00
Hand	190 weekly installments totaling	16,891.00
Arm	235 weekly installments totaling	20,891.50
Leg...............	200 weekly installments totaling	17,780.00
One testicle........	50 weekly installments totaling	4,445.00
Two testicles	150 weekly installments totaling	13,335.00

—Quoted from *Blue Collar* by Charles
Spencer, Lakeside Charter Banks, 1977

"I worked as cleanup man [in a cotton mill].
. . . They started giving us those little face
masks, but . . . the stuff would be pouring
down in lumps and that mask wouldn't last
long so you couldn't breathe through that
and you had to put it down. . . . The cotton
on the floor was over six inches deep. You
couldn't see across the room. . . . I just
couldn't make it by coughing it up and
coughing all the time. I just got so short-
winded I couldn't do the work they were
having me do. . . . And when I got home I
wasn't good for nothing."

—Walter Jones,
brown lung victim,
quoted in
Rise Gonna Rise by
Mimi Conway,
Anchor/
Doubleday, 1979

This song is written for the melody line plus two harmony and two rhythm lines. We regret space does not allow us to reproduce all five parts as published.

• MORE THAN A PAYCHECK •

by Ysaye M. Barnwell

With a reggae beat (♩ = 152)

We bring more than a pay - check to our loved ones_ and fam - 'lies;_ We bring more than a pay - check to_ our loved ones_ and fam - 'lies._

(Repeat four times)

I want - ed more_____ pay, ___ but what I've got to - day_____ Is more than I bar - gained_ for_ ____ when I walked through your_ door. ___ I bring home as - bes - to - sis, ___ sil - i - co - sis, ___

brown lung,— black— lung— dis - ease; and ra - di - a - tion—

Fine

hits the chil - dren— be - fore they've real - ly been— con - ceived.

2. Well, now, work - ers, lend— an ear,———— 'cause it's im -

por - tant that— you know— With ev - 'ry job there is— the fear—

———— that dis - ease will take— its toll.— If not dis -

ease, then in - jur - y———— may be - fall— your lot,

and if not in - jur - y,— then stress is gon - na

D.S.

tie you up— in knots. So we bring home

"The youngest child   Treated unfairly
Given freedom   Will fight back"
Will sing   —Sy Kahn, *History of Activism*
The youngest child   *Through Song*

• RISE AGAIN •

by Tom Juravich

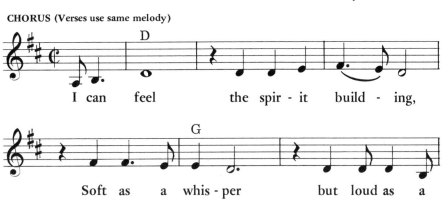

CHORUS (Verses use same melody)

I can   feel   the spir - it   build - ing,

Soft   as   a   whis - per   but   loud   as   a

roar. I can feel some-thing a-stir-ring,— Like I nev-er have— be-fore.— We've been qui-et—— too long, my friends, But the work-ing folks of this coun--try will rise— a-gain.——

1. We've been quiet for thirty years now—
You had the work, and you gave us the pay;
But with hard times 'round the corner,
You think we've seen our better day.
But we're not going back to where we began,
'Cause the working folks of this country will
   rise again.

     REPEAT CHORUS

2. Now, you say that you don't need me
And you lay me off: no work, you say.
You expect to see my head a-hanging
As I pack and walk away.
But with my brothers and sisters, so proudly
   we'll stand

As the working folks of this country rise
   again.

     REPEAT CHORUS

3. And I've heard tell of Big Bill Haywood
And Elizabeth Gurley Flynn.
They were old-time union warriors,
Gave no thought to giving in.
We will rekindle that spirit again
As the working folks of this country rise
   again.

     REPEAT CHORUS

• SMALL BUSINESS BLUES •

by Howard Bursen

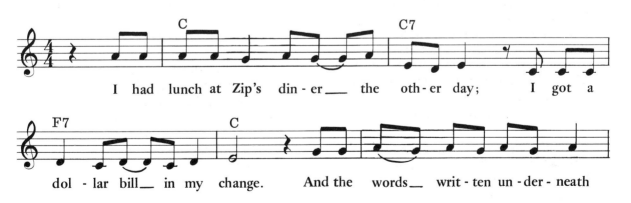

I had lunch at Zip's din - er __ the oth - er day; I got a
dol - lar bill __ in my change. And the words __ writ - ten un - der - neath

old George -'s pic - ture, well, they made me feel sad and strange.

They said, "Good luck, Joe," and down be - low, it said, "We

wish you all of the best." Seems like

Joe's out of luck and his ver - y first buck's gone

down the drain with the rest. First dol - lar on the wall

makes you feel like stand - ing tall. You got the

fu - ture in your hand proud to be a

cit - i - zen of this land. Then they put in a mall, sell - ing

all kinds of junk like stamped-out plas - tic shoes, And the

hard - work - ing folks watch their bus -'ness go broke.___ We got the
small - bus -'ness___ blues.___ Don't say A - mer - i - ca's___ gone
la - zy ___ it's the e - con - o - my's___ gone
cra - zy,___ And if we don't make a change, we're gon - na lose.___
We got the small - bus -'ness___ blues.___

2. Now, I was down in a textile-printing plant,
    makin' lots of money, back in 'sixty-eight.
By 'seventy-five we doubled production,
    but the banks said, "You're too late."
Three hundred families thrown out of
    work—
    shut down by a plant overseas.
I don't know who owns that foreign
    sweatshop,
    but the locks have American keys.

CHORUS:
First dollar on the wall
    makes you feel like standing tall.
You got the future in your hand—
    proud to be a citizen of this land.
They're squeezing the small people right out
    of business
    in the name of free enterprise.
There's ten million folks out of work today
    while the corporate skyscrapers rise.
Don't say America's gone lazy;
    it's the economy's gone crazy,

And if we don't make a change, we're gonna
    lose.
    We got the small business blues.

*(Now's a good time for an instrumental
    break—or whistle the melody.)*

CHORUS:
First dollar on the wall
    makes you feel like standing tall.
You got the future in your hand—
    proud to be a citizen of this land.
We used to be farmers, mechanics, and
    builders,
    making houses out of local white pine.
Now we're all sweeping floors in the
    shopping malls,
    standing in food-stamp lines.
Don't say America's gone lazy;
    it's the economy's gone crazy,
And if we don't make a change we're gonna
    lose.
    We got the small business blues.

• SOLIDARITY! •

by Billy Brown

Disco beat

INTRO.

It's a bird— *No!*__ It's a plane— *No!*__ It's the

hatch-et man.__ Watch out, y'all__ he's got a

hatch-et in__ his hand;__ he's chop-ping ev-'ry-thing he can.

CHORUS

So let's keep our Sol - i - dar - i - ty, let's keep our

Sol - i - dar - i - ty— Sol - i - dar - i - ty—

Let's keep our Sol - i - dar - i - ty!

VERSE

You know what we had to say a - bout the

way Mis - ter Rea - gan thinks.__ You

"I'M UNION—Darn Proud of it!"
—Placard, Sheet Metal Workers Local 102,
Washington, D.C.

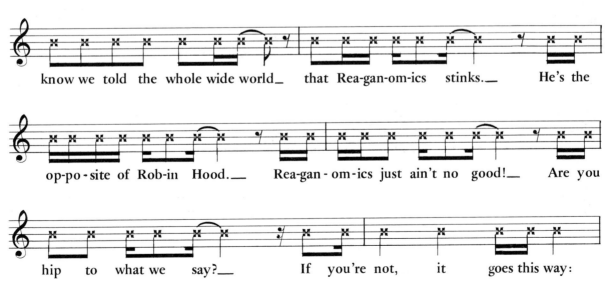

know we told the whole wide world___ that Rea-gan-om-ics stinks.___ He's the

op-po-site of Rob-in Hood.___ Rea-gan-om-ics just ain't no good!___ Are you

hip to what we say?___ If you're not, it goes this way:

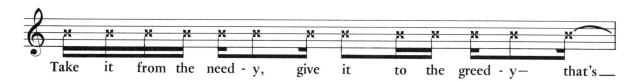

Take it from the need-y, give it to the greed-y— that's

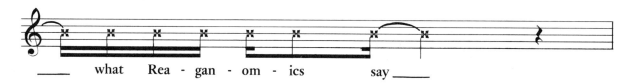

what Rea-gan-om-ics say

(To Chorus)

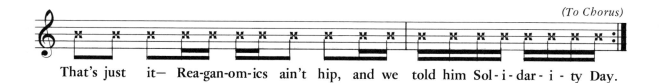

That's just it— Rea-gan-om-ics ain't hip, and we told him Sol-i-dar-i-ty Day.

2. You thought he was your friend,
   so you helped him get in.
But didn't you really know
   that you reap what you sow?
'Cause now you're out of a job,
   and you're takin' it kind of hard.
Are you hip to what we say?
   If you're not, it goes this way:
"Take it from the needy, give it to the
     greedy"—
   That's what Reaganomics say.
That's just it—Reaganomics ain't hip;
   and we told him Solidarity Day.
           CHORUS

3. We say, Hey there, Congressmen!
   Do you seriously want to stay in?
'Cause if you don't put away your knife,
   we're gonna send you back to private life.
Hey, Congressmen, hear our screams.
   We don't want his jelly beans!
Are you hip to what we say?
   If you're not, it goes this way:
"Take it from the needy, give it to the
     greedy"—
   That's what Reaganomics say.
That's just it—Reaganomics ain't hip;
   and we told him Solidarity Day.
           CHORUS

The judge asked me, "What's your name?"

"Darity," says I. "Sol I. Darity."

EPILOGUE

Hunger is bad.
Hunger is like a lion.
—African poem
of Rangi people

Big Bill Haywood, the Wobbly organizer, would stand in front of a crowd waggling all the fingers of one hand in the air. "Once," he would say, "this was us! Separate and weak." Then he would boom, "But now, with a union—*this* is us!" And he would draw his fingers together into a fist.

With unity, union and a century of hard work, American working people have won an eight-hour day, more pay, better work conditions, public education, and personal dignity. But with every step forward there has been another half-step back.

We work eight hours a day, but nonunion workers still put in ten and twelve hours a day. We have won safety measures; but American firms manufacture their poisons in places like India. Our children are out of the mills and in schools; but in Korea, American firms employ nine- and 10-year-olds full time. We have dignity, until the firm moves to Taiwan or Venezuela, where it can pay fifty cents an hour.

As our earth draws together, no improvement in quality of work or quality of life can last unless it touches the whole world.

"The labor question is the same the world over, and laborers of the world should clasp hands for their common weal."
  —Frank K. Foster at founding
    convention of A.F.L., 1884

"The working people know no country. They are citizens of the world."
  —Samuel Gompers, president,
    A.F.L., 1910

"Life was softened by a great equality. All the tasks of women—cooking, caring for children, tanning, and sewing—were considered dignified and worthwhile. No work was looked upon as menial. Consequently, there were no menial jobs."

— Sioux Indian, quoted in *Children of the Wild West* by Russell Freedman, Houghton Mifflin, 1983

• SOMOS EL BARCO/WE ARE THE BOAT •

by Lorre Wyatt

Moderately

CHORUS

2. Now, the boat we are sailing in was built by
    many hands,
   And the sea we are sailing on, it touches
    every sand.

CHORUS

3. Oh, the voyage has been long and hard, and
    yet we're sailing still,
   With a song to help us pull together, if we
    only will.

CHORUS

4. So with our hopes we raise the sails to face
    the winds once more,
   And with our hearts we chart the waters
    never sailed before.

CHORUS

Spanish translation by Salvador Ten and David
Shea:

CHORUS

   Somos el barco, somos el mar,
   Yo navego en ti, tú navegas en mí,

We are the boat, we are the sea,
I sail in you, you sail in me.

1. El arroyo le canta al río.
   El río le canta al mar;
   Y el mar le canta al barco
   Que lejos nos va a llevar.

CHORUS

2. El barco en que navegamos
   Fué hecho por muchas manos,
   Y el mar que ahora surcamos
   Muchas tierras tocará.

CHORUS

3. La jornade ha sido dura
   Y aún seguimos navegando,
   Desafiando las tormentas
   Y así siempre seguiremos.

CHORUS

4. Con nuestras esperanzas
   Altas velas levantamos,
   Y con nuestros corazones
   Nuevas rutas exploramos.

CHORUS

Divisions in the house of labor? Perish the thought. But unions fought over everything —tactics, politics, whether or not they would admit ethnic groups or women or people of color. In the 1880s the Knights of Labor and the newly formed American Federation of Labor were hardly on speaking terms. Thirty years later, the Industrial Workers of the World (Wobblies) sneered at the A.F.L., while Eugene Debs and his Socialists laughed at them both. At the turn of the century, eight major unions had written into their charters: "white only." In 1980 one union in Boston had two separate locals—one for Irish-Americans and one for Italian-Americans.

In the 1930s the Socialist unions and the Communist unions and the conservative unions attacked each other with song parodies like:

The Cloak-makers' Union is a no-good union. It's a company union for the bosses.

The main divisions are between the skilled tradespeople—the "aristocrats of labor"— and the unskilled and unemployed. These are the ancient lines dividing the human race.

According to *Black Enterprise* magazine, some unions "continue to operate as if they were medieval guilds, passing jobs from father to son or even from uncle to nephew or buddy to buddy rather than opening membership to minorities. . . . Jobs for [minorities] remain elusive after 20 years of Civil Rights laws, executive orders, presidential directives and special task forces. . . ." ("Blood, Sweat, and Steel," May 1984)

To paraphrase Hamlet:

To fight, perchance to win, aye there's the rub.
For victory brings power and prestige.
And the children of the children of the fighters
Take all for granted and, in turn, oppress.

The labor movement has fought, and always, eventually, it has come together again. Today, as the world draws closer and closer together, the search for unity and union widens to encompass the entire planet.

—P.S.

"We want the job security found in
   Japan . . .
We want the strong voice in management
   found in Germany . . .
We want the rational industrial policies
   found in Sweden . . .
We want the decent wages found in the
   United States and Canada . . .
We want the fighting spirit found in Brazil
   and South Africa . . .

"The question of international solidarity is no longer a simple moral question. Without that solidarity, we will be outclassed and outfought."
—Owen Bieber, president, U.A.W.

• CARRY IT ON •

by Gil Turner
Additional words by Marion Wade

There's a man by my side walk-in'. There's a voice in-side me talk-in'. There's a word needs a say-in':___

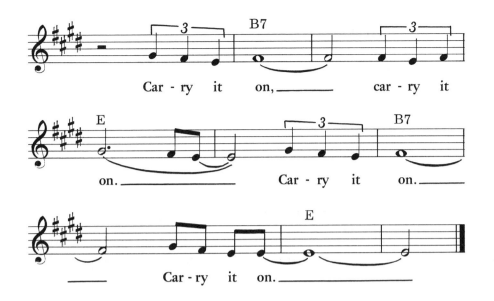

Car - ry it on,_____ car - ry it

on._____ Car - ry it on._____

_____ Car - ry it on._____

2. Through the air the song is winging.
   Down the years, hope keeps springing.
   No more tears! We're still singing
   Carry it on . . . Carry it on.

3. If you can't go on any longer,
   Take the hand of your sister and brother.
   Every victory gonna bring another!
   Carry it on . . . Carry it on.

To all living things, happiness.
—Hindu prayer

HINTS FOR PERFORMING THE SONGS IN THIS BOOK

Most of the songs in this book were made up by ordinary people, and any ordinary person who likes to sing should be able to sing them. It would help if you keep in mind the particular tradition the song comes from —whether it's Irish-American or Afro-American or Slovakian-American and so on.

Some songs can be sung with no accompaniment. Some songs would sound great if they had a whole orchestra behind them. But quite often you can do very well with a little bit of rhythm from a drum or guitar, or whatever is handy. In any case, remember to get the words out clearly.

We have pitched every song in what we think is a convenient key for the average person; but sometimes you can get a more powerful effect if you raise the key higher. On the other hand, a growly bass or an alto would prefer to put the song lower than we have written it.

A good singer will usually change the melody or rhythm slightly to make it suit his or her voice. For example, on page 99 is Mimi Fariña's fine melody for "Bread and Roses." Compare this with the way Frayda Bluestein sings it (with dancing mandolin, Autoharp, banjo, fiddle, and guitar accompaniment) on the great Bluestein Family LP *Travelin' Blues* (Swallow Records, 434 E. Main St., Ville Platte, LA 70586):

If you have a number of people who sing together well enough for a chorus but you're not sure who is good enough to be a soloist, try having two or three sing unison on the verses and then have the rest sing the refrain. It is usually hard to get the words clearly understood if more than two or three are singing verses together.

If you are making a presentation on the stage, you might consider (after getting such photographic and performance permissions as are necessary) photographing some of the pictures in this book and then projecting the image with a slide projector. This will help bring the songs to life. If it is a long story-song, sometimes a group of actors can mime the action described while someon is singing the song.

Sometimes you can have a narrator working along with the singers and a few spoken words can frame the song in its historical period.

Give thought and discussion to choosing the exactly right songs. There's never time enough to sing all the songs you want to sing; picking the right one is important. Beware of singing just one verse of a song and one verse of another. Usually you should stick to a song long enough to really get "into it." When a crowd of people get to know a song, they will sing the chorus so well that they inspire themselves.

And when they can inspire themselves, they will inspire others.

—P.S.

HOW THIS BOOK CAME TO BE

In 1982, Pete Seeger wrote in *Sing Out,* a small folk-music magazine, that few Americans realized how the labor movement began in this country. Even union members knew little about the events in Chicago that triggered the development of unions around the world. In 1886, dozens of people died at Haymarket Square. Afterward, four men were hanged. Their crime was advocating an eight-hour workday.

As a result of Pete's article, a group of us came together to put out a songbook that would commemorate the Haymarket Affair and celebrate working people and the growth of unions.

Pete Seeger and Bob Reiser wound up with the job of writing the book. But before that, the committee made some important decisions. We searched through hundreds of the best work and union songs of the last 200 years, and somehow managed to trim the field. Some great songs had to be left out (many) and some great songwriters are unrepresented (Malvina Reynolds and others). Since we wanted the book to reach every interested person—not just those who could read music—we made it a picture book as well.

After payments to songwriters, artists, agents, editors, printers, proofreaders, papermakers, and the army of people involved in getting out this book, we hope there will still be some royalties coming in during future years. Since the committee did not do this book to get rich, half of the money will go to such groups as The Labor Heritage Foundation, *Sing Out* magazine, the Illinois Labor Historical Association, and *Talkin' Union* magazine.

If we can inspire a deeper love for the hard-working people of past generations and encourage future generations not to run away from problems, but to dig in and try to solve them, we'll feel repaid.

In 1890 Sam Gompers urged the world labor movement to make May 1st a day to commemorate the Haymarket dead. Perhaps this book will encourage people to put on musical programs, occasions for people of all ages to get together and listen to music that has reached around the world, touching friends and fellow working people on every continent and island.

MIKE GLICK, NGOMA AND JARIBU HILL, JUDY GORMAN JACOBS, BOBBIE MCGEE, BOB REISER, JO SCHWARTZ, PETE SEEGER, JON STEIN, RUTH STRECKER, NED TREANOR, MARION WADE

Some Further Reading . . .

Blue Collar: An Internal Examination of the Workplace, by Charles Spencer, Lakeside-Charter Books, Box 7651, Chicago, 1977. First-hand account from a 25-year steel worker.

Forty Acres: Cesar Chavez and the Farm Workers, by Mark Day, Praeger, 1971.

The Haymarket Tragedy, by Paul Avrich, Princeton University Press, 1984.

History of the Labor Movement in the United States, by Philip S. Foner, International Pubs. Co., 1947–82. Classic six-volume history of labor.

Labor in America, by M. B. Schnapper, Public Affairs Press, 1972. An illustrated history.

Lawrence 1912: The Bread & Roses Strike, by William Cahn, Pilgrim, 1980.

Making Our Way, by William L. and Jacqueline H. Katz, Dial, 1975. First-person accounts by working people around 1900.

Pictorial History of American Labor, by William Cahn, Crown, 1972. Working people in the U.S. from Colonial times to 1970.

Rebel Voices: An I.W.W. Anthology, by Joyce Kornbluth, University of Michigan Press, 1964.

Rise Gonna Rise: A Portrait of Southern Textile Workers, by Mimi Conway, with photos by Earl Dotter, Anchor/Doubleday, 1979.

So Long Partner, by Fred Wright, UE Publications, 11 E. 51st St., New York. Anthology of Fred Wright's labor cartoons, 1950–80.

Talkin' Union, the newsletter of labor music, lore, and history. Subscriptions: $6.50/year. Box 5349, Takoma Park, Md. 20912.

Voices from the Mountain, by Guy and Candide Carawan, Knopf, 1975. Photos, songs, interviews with Appalachian coal miners, 1930 to the present.

We Be Here When the Morning Comes, by Woolley and Reid, University Press of Kentucky, 1975. The coal wars of the 1970s.

Working, by Studs Terkel, Pantheon, 1974.

. . . and Listening:

Somebody's Story, by Charlie King, Rainbow Snake Records, 94 N. Leverett Rd., Leverett, Mass. 01054.

Steve and Peter Jones, Clouds Records, 6607 Marywood Rd., Bethesda, Md. 20817.

Travelin' Blues ("Bread & Roses"), by the Bluestein Family, Swallow Records, 434 E. Main St., Ville Platte, La. 70586.

Recordings of Si Kahn, Joe Glazer, and Larry Penn on Collector Records, 1604 Arbor View Rd., Silver Spring, Md. 20902.

Recordings of Tom Juravich, UAW Records, 111 South Rd., Box 432, Farmington, Conn. 06032.

Index of Songs

Photo Credits

Amalgamated Clothing Workers, pages 45, 86, 92, 94, 99, 123, 143, 177.

Henri Carter Bresson (Magnum Photos), page 178.

Catholic University of America, page 53.

CBS Television, page 210.

Robert Cooper, page 224.

Denver Public Library, page 30.

The Detroit News, page 131.

Earl Dotter, pages 6, 187, 194, 196, 206, 219, 222, 226, 229, 230, 232, 235, 241, 250.

Every Saturday, March 1871, page 49.

Ford Library, page 124.

Paul Fusco (Magnum Photos), page 212.

Hansel Meith Hagel, page 249.

Ken Hyman, pages 129, 204, 243, 244.

I.L.G.W.U., pages 48, 88, 170, 171, 172, 189, 197.

Labadie Collection, University of Michigan, pages 102, 104, 110, 138.

Library of Congress, pages 6, 24, 26, 29, 34, 45, 47, 50, 55, 56, 57, 60, 64, 67, 68, 69, 70, 72, 77, 78, 132, 135, 140, 157.

Library of Congress, Jack Delano, page 161.

Library of Congress, Hine Collection, pages 89, 91.

Library of Congress, Lange, pages 134, 144, 168.

Library of Congress, Parks, page 147.

Library of Congress, Rothstein, page 154.

Library of Congress, John Vachon, pages 126, 167.

Manos (Magnum Photos), page 97.

Museum of the American Indian, page 14.

Museum of the City of New York, page 46.

Nebraska Historical Society, page 18.

Newspaper Guild of New York, Local #3, pages 174, 176, 220.

New York Historical Society, pages 38, 43.

New York University Library, Tamiment Collection, pages 84, 116, 117.

Oakland Museum, Dorothea Lange, pages 152, 158.

Bob Reiser, pages 110, 163, 237.

Milton Rogovin, page 183.

Naomi and Walter Rosenblum, pages 80, 115.

Salmons, The Burlington Strike, pages 106, 108.

Bill Strode, page 202.

Taxi Drivers and Allied Workers, Local #3036, page 215.

Sandi Thacker, pages 6, 198, 199.

U.A.W., pages 32, 150.

United Electrical, Radio, and Machine Workers, pages 101, 180.

United Mine Workers, page 74.

University of Louisville, page 76.

Valentine Museum, Richmond, Va., page 82.

Wayne State Labor Archives, pages 13, 16, 22, 27, 36, 40, 113, 136, 138.

Wide World Photos, page 164.

William J. Olsen Studios, Milwaukee, WI, page 253.

Robert Yellin, page 121.